# I Prayed, He Answered

## William L. Vaswig

Foreword by Agnes Sanford

AUGSBURG PUBLISHING HOUSE
MINNEAPOLIS, MINNESOTA

I PRAYED, HE ANSWERED

Copyright © 1977 Augsburg Publishing House

Library of Congress Catalog Card No. 77-72457

International Standard Book No. 0-8066-1589-3

Scripture quotations unless otherwise noted are from the Revised Standard Version of the Bible, copyright 1946, 1952, and 1971 by the Division of Christian Education of the National Council of Churches. KJV refers to King James Version. NEB refers to the New English Bible, copyright 1961, 1970 by the Delegates of the Oxford University Press.

MANUFACTURED IN THE UNITED STATES OF AMERICA

To
Agnes Sanford,
the lovely lady whom God used
to touch and heal our family more than once,
with deepest affection and appreciation.

# *Contents*

# *Foreword*

This book about Christian healing is not only fascinating reading, but it is also a powerful exposition of practical theology. Pastor Vaswig clearly brings out the truth that followers of Jesus are commanded to heal the sick, and he makes many sensible suggestions for doing so. I am especially glad that his suggestions include full cooperation with the medical professionals whose healing arts, of course, all come from God.

Pastor Vaswig is beloved throughout his own church, but his approach to healing and prevailing prayer is open to all who believe in Jesus Christ as Lord, and he now travels widely holding preaching and teaching missions.

As he himself relates, his family and I have shared rich experiences of the Lord's mercy and power to heal, and I am overjoyed that by this book he is able to make his new insights into the life of the Spirit and the healing ministry even more widely known.

AGNES SANFORD

# Introduction

In a lifetime one meets perhaps one or two people who make all the difference in the world. For me and my family, Agnes Sanford is one of those people. The whole direction of our lives changed because of her.

This book is about the difference Agnes Sanford has made. In everything from theological understanding to living out God's will in Christian caring, she is a veritable gold mine of wisdom and motivation. Prayer doesn't mean the same to my family anymore —in either theory or practice.

The story that changed our lives was difficult to write because of memories rekindled. Though the memories no longer hurt, I write out of a great deal of heartbreak and pain. It is difficult indeed to bare one's soul so deeply, showing so much of the dark side of personal and family life. My son Philip unhesitatingly gave me permission to relate it all.

*I Prayed, He Answered* is a bit of witness from a man whom God touched through a woman who took him to the foothills of prayer and left him there to climb. I am deeply indebted to Agnes for most of the insights found on these pages.

I want to thank Philip, who so meticulously typed and edited a number of copies of the manuscript. Since God touched us through his illness, it seems highly appropriate that he should be the one to see it through to its final draft. How gracious he is about having his life opened up in this book.

Thanks to Marcine, my dear wife, who went through it all with me and who is primarily responsible for motivating me to write. She always believes me more çapable than I am.

And thanks to Joanna, John, Charis, Rene, and Maira, my children, who have helped me understand what a community created and maintained by the Holy Spirit is all about.

WILLIAM L. VASWIG

# *Prince Philip*

I was on one of my ego trips. I had been on many ego trips before, but this was the biggest and lasted the longest. I was committed to building the largest, most socially concerned, most evangelistic congregation in Southern California. When neighboring pastors hinted that I was "stealing their sheep," I resented it greatly and let them know that I had done nothing to encourage such moves and that their sheep were wandering into my pasture because they had chosen to do so. Inwardly, however, I knew that *I* was more effective, *ours* was a better church, and *they* were preaching a gospel inferior to the gospel I was preaching.

11

Ego trips take time and effort. This particular one took me 16 to 18 hours a day over a period of years. I was home at mealtime, and that was about all. Seldom did I spend time with my lovely wife, Marcine, or with our six children. It wasn't that I didn't love them or care for them; I was just too busy with my ego trip. I protested loudly if anyone pointed an accusing finger at me with my busy schedule. After all, I was building the kingdom of God. How dare anyone point a finger at the kingdom-builder!

The time away from home took its toll. My wife was overworked and underloved. She kept on year after year, running the house and all our finances and managing our children too. About once every year we would have a big fight about how I cared more for my church than I did for her and the kids. It was never resolved because I claimed to be caught in a trap—and I was. I had become a workaholic, enslaved to my ego trip. I was building a monster that was controlling me.

Our oldest son, Philip, was a sensitive, loving, bright boy to whom I had always felt especially close. He never insisted that I play with him much. He seemed to share with me like an adult, as early as age five. In other words, he played the game *my* way. He was willing to discuss subjects of my choosing at any time, and he would always open himself up to me. He listened attentively as I poured out to him the woes and the joys of a parish pastor on the run.

Philip developed stomach problems during his first year of high school. School was very difficult for him—not his classes, but rather his relationships with his peers. He often spoke helplessly of other students. He loved a few, but he was generally turned off by his generation. His only real interests in high school were writing and films, which he delved into with his whole heart. He published two short books of poetry.

But the stomach problems persisted and his anxiety increased. Gradually, the number of his friends dropped from three or four down to one—and finally to none. The reason? Relationships were "just too much hassle." It was too difficult to keep everything open with people, and Philip could not be casual about anything. Everything had to be on the deepest level of communication.

I often went into Philip's room late at night, only to find him still awake and in agony of body and soul. How he struggled to understand life and what was going on inside of him! Giving him the last hours of the day,

I tried to help. I listened a lot and often went to bed amazed by the mind of one who asked questions that I hadn't even thought of in my 40 years. But he was in pain and I knew it. He seemed to carry the weight of the world on his shoulders. Marcine and I prayed together for him.

One day I was called home from church. "Philip is in his bedroom," my wife told me, "and something is terribly wrong!" I hurried home, hoping he wouldn't destroy himself. "God have mercy on us! God have mercy on us!" I cried as I drove.

I found Philip on his bed up against a wall, with a knife in each hand, defending himself against enemies he believed to be in the room. After much pleading I got the knives away from him. Then he went into the bedroom closet and sat in a fetal position, crying that he never wanted to come out. When I finally coaxed him out, he put his alarm clock on the floor and smashed it with his fist. While I ran to call the doctor, Philip slashed his wrists with glass from the face of the clock.

Philip's internist said that he could do nothing, that we should take the boy to a psychiatrist immediately. We arranged for Philip to meet Dr. E. at a private psychiatric hospital in Los Angeles. I had a sinking feeling, taking one of my own into a mental hospital for the first time. As a pastor, I had visited such places before, but this was different. This was our own son, our oldest! This was my confidant, my supporter!

No one in the hospital wore a uniform. The staff was very casual—a little too casual, it seemed to me. They were very friendly, but I was worried. Then Dr. E. appeared—a walking caricature of a psychiatrist. His long, kinky hair stood out from his balding head, and his clothes looked thrown together. His manner was very deliberate, yet he was very kind and understanding.

Dr. E. said Philip should stay in the hospital. Philip refused. After some heartrending minutes, we agreed to do as the doctor advised. Two young men came to restrain Philip, and we were told to leave and not return for two days. As Marcine and I walked down the hallway, Philip cried after us with a cry I shall not forget as long as I live. "Dad!" he screamed, "I'll never forget this, Dad! I'll never forget this!"

As we drove home we had to stop every few blocks to sit and cry. I couldn't even see to drive. We asked ourselves what we had done wrong. We remembered every harsh word, every spanking, every raised voice, every overprotective moment. We groveled in self-pity and self-hate.

Philip was put into solitary confinement for the night and thereafter was heavily sedated. I thank God for anti-psychotic drugs. Though they are obviously not a cure, they help so much in reducing the evidence of psychosis.

For the next two years we were all in agony. Philip was in two private psychiatric hospitals on three different occasions. Once he broke out and called home. He said, "Dad, I am out of the hospital and I will tell you where I am so you can come and get me if you promise not to put me back in the hospital." I would half promise, hoping I could keep my word, only to witness Philip become either suicidal or homicidal, so we had to put him in the hospital again.

After Philip underwent weeks and weeks of psychotherapy, the doctors finally decided he could stay at home if he was heavily medicated. What hell that was for all of us! Even on a strong, constant dose of drugs he would lose his temper at the slightest provocation. His four sisters and one brother lived in almost constant fear and dread of him. Philip became extremely defensive of us, to the point of wanting to kill anyone from the church who criticized us. Our parish did not know of his illness.

Months and months of tears and fears wore us all down. We became supersensitive, supercritical, hostile, and defensive. We often became very angry with Philip, but, afraid to say anything to him, we took our anger out on one another. Several times when Philip was not present, his brother John flew into a rage because he could not understand the why of it all. When we finally realized how much anger we had inside because of Philip's condition, we became more understanding and helpful to one another.

The doctors confided to me that Philip would probably never be entirely well, and only after eight to ten years of weekly psychotherapy would he even get better. At one time we even prayed that if God wanted to, he should take Philip.

The day we had taken Philip to the hospital for the first time, Pastor George called. He told us his own son had been diagnosed that very day as having cancer. We pleaded with God to spare their son and take ours. Months later their son died and our son continued to live, though he was a zombie, out of touch with reality. We asked God, "Why?"

We wrote to our pastor friends and asked

them to pray. Most of them wrote encouraging letters telling us they were holding Philip up before God daily. Our good district president, Dr. Gaylerd Falde, came to our home and wept with us. His assistant, Dr. Cornils, came and sat with us and shared our troubles—but no one could lift the burden.

The doctors tried vitamin therapy in addition to regular psychotherapy. They considered using electroshock treatments, but at the last moment decided against it. They also put Philip on lithium carbonate — the only drug useful with some forms of mental illness. It helped to some extent, but the problem was still very much there. Philip slept during the day and walked around at night. At times he would stand up for two hours outside our bedroom door in the middle of the night, while Marcine and I lay wondering what he would do next.

The doctors hesitantly diagnosed Philip as paranoid schizophrenic. The diagnosis was supported by a number of people in the psychiatric community. And they came to an additional conclusion which I found very hard to handle.

The doctors told me, in a kindly way but in no uncertain terms, that I was the heavy weight in Philip's problem. They suspected that, because I was a pastor, my children saw me not as an ordinary father, but as God's representative. This was especially true of Philip, because he was extremely sensitive. Instead of telling me to "go to hell" as other teenagers might have done, Philip kept all his anger within. The doctors said it had actually changed the chemistry of his brain. To oversimplify, what I heard from them was that my being a minister had driven my son crazy. I was hounded by the thought that if I was the "heavy weight" in Philip's case, surely I was the no-good father I had never admitted being, but which I secretly feared I was.

In communicating God to people, I had communicated to our children a God whose representative *I* had become, and one whom they surely were in no position to rebel against. How do you talk back to a powerful father when God stands directly behind him? Even if it is perfectly justifiable, even if he is wrong, do you dare talk back to a man who represents God? Philip could not, and holding rebellion inside had literally driven him out of his mind—at least that's what the doctors concluded.

What do you do when you suddenly become painfully aware that, in your self-centered egotism, you have caused your own son to go crazy? I kicked the walls. I cried for days. I laid my head on my desk at work and sank into depression. I twice planned in great detail how to take my own life. I railed at God. I shook my fists at him. What kind of God could possibly permit the son of one of his own servants to lose his mind? "It's not fair!" I cried. I told God I hated him. I cursed him. I blamed him outright. I looked for other scapegoats too, and I lived in misery for weeks on end.

One day Marcine mentioned *The Healing Light* by Agnes Sanford, a book I had read years before while at the seminary. Marcine asked if I thought we should try to get in touch with this woman, though we had no idea where she lived. I had not been much impressed with the book, but we were desperate, so I agreed to try to locate the author. After many unsuccessful attempts, we learned that she lived in our own city, Los Angeles, about an hour's drive from our home. The only address we had was a post office box number we had obtained from a recording firm which had taped some of her lectures. I wrote to Agnes and told her the story.

Dear Mrs. Sanford,

I am writing you concerning my 18-year-old son, whom the psychiatrists designate "paranoid schizophrenic," to find out if it would be possible for you either to see our son or to pray for him in your private devotions.

Philip is the oldest of six children. He has always been a sensitive child. He is very bright and really only showed signs of illness during the last year or so. Psychiatrists seem to think that I, his father, am the "heavy weight" in the problem. He finds it impossible to express normal anger to me because he cannot separate pastor-father from father. We have an excellent relationship—from one point of view—and almost *too good* from another. I cried for two days when I heard about my part in this illness.

But the problem involves not only his father, but also his peers and people in the church. This illness, as the doctors diagnose it (U.C.L.A. + two or three other psychiatrists), consists in this — that his thinking process is way ahead of his emotional development. He's 18 emotionally and about 23 intellectually.

Our whole congregation has been in prayer for Philip, who is a Christian and who is seeking wholeness. Forty-eight people remember him each morning at 5:30 in prayer in the "Brave Christian" program.

In our Christmas letter to hundreds we explained the nature of Philip's illness, and we have received promises to pray from all over the country.

The board of deacons of our church and their wives met one evening in our home and prayed with him also, but no positive answer yet.

He continues to be under weekly psychotherapy and is presently, in addition, under chemotherapy. He also takes 31 vitamin pills daily including B3, B6, and C. The vitamin therapy is called "Mega-Vitamin Therapy" and offers some hope to change the brain chemistry.

Philip is tremendously talented, having published poems and written film scripts. His best friend just found Christ, so he is presently happy over that. He is at home and is pleasant and cooperative. When he goes off the medication, he becomes tremendously anxious, but really never loses touch with *who* he is. His behavior has become psychotic two or three times.

We believe God is setting the stage in his own time and good way to heal the young man. The psychiatrists tell us it will be eight to ten years before he will be well. My wife and I don't believe the doctors are God, though we think God uses them.

Is it possible that we could bring Philip to see you, Agnes, so you could pray for the healing of his memories? Our hearts are leaning that way more and more over the months, as hundreds pray. We think God can use you to touch him. Will you let us come?

> In Christ's bonds,
> Bill and Marcine Vaswig

One day I received a typed letter on simple paper from Agnes, saying that she thought she could help our son, but that it might mean giving up psychiatrists and medication. She said I could call her and make an appointment to bring Philip to her home. Here is her letter:

Dear Mr. Vaswig,

Yes, I do feel that I should see your son and that God can help him through me. The only trouble is, there are too many praying people and psychiatrists involved. Please do not tell anyone he is coming to see me—not until afterwards —then we can consult about it. And of course you must be willing when I dare to suggest it to let him give up his psychiatrists for the two do not go together. I won't suggest it however right in the beginning and not unless he wants it.

I don't believe you are the cause of his trouble. Psychiatrists always say that it is either the father or the mother when they don't know what else to say.

As for arranging a time to see him, I will have to trust you with my telephone number. Please do not give it to anyone else nor tell anyone that you have it!

With all best wishes,
Agnes Sanford

The letter was like a shaft of light in a very dark existence. While I was not at all convinced she could do anything, I had the faint hope that maybe, somehow, she could. We asked Philip if he would like to go see a lady who was very powerful in prayer and who might be able to help him, and he agreed.

On Friday of that very week, Philip and I left for Agnes Sanford's home. Philip was quiet. He had taken his regular dose of medicine that day. We arrived at a beautiful home, peacefully located on a hill overlooking a valley. We rang the bell. I had expected a large, imposing woman. Instead she was small and no longer young, with graying hair and a friendly smile. In a pleasant voice, she invited us in.

"Hello, Philip," she said. "Don't be afraid." I will never forget those first words. Apparently she knew immediately how to treat a person who was very sick.

"Well now," she said quickly, "pastor, why don't you go down the hall to the first door on the right, and Philip and I will go downstairs to my study. Would that be all right Philip?" Philip uttered a faint yes and I walked down the hall while he and Agnes walked down the carpeted stairs to her study. I was emotionally drained, and as soon as I sat down I fell asleep. A short time later Agnes bustled into the room.

"Well now," she began, "this must be very hard on you as a father." I burst into tears.

"Oh, if you only knew," I said.

"I prayed for Philip downstairs," Agnes went on, "and I told him he could stay down there as long as he liked. I prayed for the healing of his memories and for the release from the spirit of fear that has been holding him. Philip will be better, but now I think perhaps I should pray for you too."

Pray for me? I'm an ordained clergyman. The last time anyone had put hands on me in prayer was when I was ordained 20 years before. "I'm not sure about that," I thought to myself. Still, I wanted so badly to be released from my feelings of guilt and anger and resentment against God, that I consented.

Agnes placed her hands on my head and prayed a prayer I will never forget. She asked God to remove the awful heaviness from me. She told God, in very down-to-earth language, that she believed I was not the cause of the problem and that sometimes psychiatrists blame parents when they don't know who else to blame. But, she went on, "Whether he caused it in any way, Lord, that is not important. The important thing is that right now he can be released from it."

Her words released me! All the hideous

guilt came tumbling out like spilled water on a floor. *God touched me!* I met the God of grace. I started to cry again, and soon I was sobbing like a baby—sobs of relief. The burden was lifted. For the first time in months, I was seeing the light at the end of the tunnel.

On the way home Philip suddenly asked me to stop the car. He opened the door and vomited in the street. We were later to discover the deep meaning of that action. As we made our way home I kept thinking, "If God used Agnes to help me so much, I wonder what she has done for Philip." But there was no sign of any change in him.

The next day, however, Philip made his bed for the first time in two years. We got excited, but then we cooled off. We had been hopeful many times before, only to be disappointed. Now we were very cautious. Yet, day after day, we noticed changes taking place in Philip. Agnes prayed for him again five days later, then again in two weeks, in a month, and a few times in the following six months. Though he had stopped seeing his psychiatrist, in three months Philip seemed to be newly healed!

We asked Agnes in more detail what she had prayed for him. She said that she com-

manded the fear to leave Philip. The Bible
says, "Perfect love casts out fear." Since the
cross was the best picture of perfect love she
knew, she asked Philip to concentrate on the
image of the cross. Then she commanded the
fears to leave, and she asked the love of Christ
to fill Philip.

Agnes said she saw that Philip was much
more sensitive than most people, and that
he had picked up a good deal of fear at the
time of the earthquake in Southern California. (It was about that time that Philip began
to show signs of psychosis.) Agnes explained
that Jesus, who is not bound by space or
time, could go back in Philip's mind and heal
any painful memories, from his prenatal state
to the present. When Philip recalled the past
pain would no longer be connected with his
memories. We were amazed!

We were eager to see if Philip really was
getting better or if it was just our wishful
thinking. About a month after Agnes prayed
for him, I asked her if it would be all right to
take Philip back to the psychiatrist. She replied that it was perfectly all right and that
she was anxious to hear what the doctors
had to say.

I dropped Philip off at the hospital and

headed back to my office. I prayed that if there was a change and he was being healed, the doctors would see it and say so. Shortly, the phone rang.

"What's going on, Bill?" Dr. E. asked. I hesitated, but finally got courage enough to tell him that an old woman had prayed for Philip. He wanted more details. We met for lunch and I told him everything that had happened.

"This woman surely didn't do him any harm," he said. "And she sure knows a good deal about psychiatry. Philip is much better. I have taken him off two-thirds of his medication today."

I jumped in, "But how do you know, doctor?"

"Though I'm eclectic, I'm also a Freudian analyst," he replied, "and I have been analyzing Philip's dreams for two years. They have completely changed."

I was overjoyed! Now we knew for certain that Philip was being healed. The darkest days were finally over!

Six months after Philip's first visit to see Agnes Sanford, Dr. E. wrote the following letter to the director of admissions at a college Philip hoped to attend:

Dear Sir:

Philip Vaswig has been under my care for the past 18 months for emotional problems. He was discharged from my care two months ago, having completely recovered. Mr. Vaswig is a stable, intelligent, entirely competent young man and should have no difficulty with college level work.

Sincerely,
E., M.D.

A few weeks later, Philip and I met with a group of psychiatrists, psychologists, and psychiatric social workers (including a former president of the American Psychiatric Association) at the clinic Dr. E. directs. Philip's case history was presented to those attending:

Patient is a 19-year-old male, oldest son of a minister. He was quite withdrawn as a child and was obsessive about many things. In his mid-teens he became increasingly withdrawn and resentful and exhibited ideas of reference, grandiosity, and persecution symptoms.

Also, at this time, he developed a great deal of stomach and upper gastric distress and was having several severe attacks per day, which were relieved by antacids and Valium. X-ray studies revealed some evidence of gastritis.

His father has a large congregation in the Valley. The family is very intelligent and achievement oriented. The parents are both supportive but are increasingly more distressed because of his illness.

A few months preceding his first hospitalization, P.V.'s symptoms became more severe and it was recommended that he be removed from school. He was exhibiting acting-out behavior including excessive drinking. It was arranged for him to be taught at home by Tele-Teach, which further increased his isolation. He was referred to a psychologist in Orange County by whom he was treated with psychotherapy. His condition continued to get worse, however, and before admission he threatened to attack people and also threatened to injure himself with a knife. He also began to report hallucinations.

### 1st Hospitalization 5/18/71 to 6/5/71

Patient was very resentful of being placed in the hospital at first but responded very rapidly to psychotherapy, milieu therapy, and medication, especially Haldol. It seemed to be beneficial also to be separated from his home environment. He became increasingly cooperative and his abdominal symptoms became less severe and then disappeared during his hospital stay. He began to socialize more and became interested in other activities. It is apparent that he is of superior intelligence. Upon discharge he stated he was willing to continue in psychotherapy and willing to continue taking his medication. His improvement during this hospitalization was remarkable.

### 2nd Hospitalization 10/5/71 to 10/7/71

Prior to this hospitalization, patient was seen in the office in an agitated, delusional state. He had been seen several days previous to this visit and at that time was doing extremely well both in school and at his part-time job. He also had been writing poetry and was involved in film making. However, he called and said that paranoia was rearing its head and requested emergency help.

At this time his affect was grossly inappropriate and very labile. He shifted from grinning and euphoria to deep depression. He was phobic about going out. His judgment and insight were poor and he had feelings of grandiosity, delusions, and ideas of reference. The treatment in the hospital consisted of medication and psychotherapy.

After discharge the patient was supposed to return to school, but was unable to achieve this. He again developed severe gastric complaints. His progression was downhill and he cut off his associations with his friends and became increasingly withdrawn at home. His mood became very labile and he threatened suicide often. His threats of suicide appeared serious and he was admitted to the hospital a third time for definitive treatment.

### 3rd Hospitalization 11/15/71 to 11/26/71

Observation, milieu therapy, and psychotherapy were prescribed. ECT was considered. P.V. left the hospital with the help of his girl friend when Dr. E. was on vacation and refused to come back. His condition appeared to have improved, however, and it was intended to continue following him in outpatient treatment.

At one point in his history, which P.V. says was subsequent to his last hospitalization, his father took him to a faith healer which resulted in a dramatic change in patient's behavior.

### 9/13/73 (Office Visit)

P.V. is looking for a job. He is oriented and calm with appropriate affect but somewhat distant as though in a world of his own. He stated he does not want to be hospitalized again in the future and feels he is capable of controlling his emotions and behavior so that won't be necessary. However, he is not entirely sure he wants to control his thoughts all the time as he enjoys being on a different plane than others are. His fantasy life has vastly increased lately. P.V. says he wishes to pursue a career in writing. His insight and judgment are good.

After the case history was read, Philip and I were questioned by the doctors and staff for two hours, question after question.

When the time came to end the interview, Dr. B., former president of the American Psychiatric Association, said, "I have two comments to make. First, we have been watching you both during this interview and we noticed that each time you speak, Philip, your father gets a gleam in his eyes and that each time he speaks, you get a gleam in your eye. We'd like to congratulate you on your relationship to your father.

"The second statement I'd like to make is that you are a very fortunate young man, Philip, to have ever run across that 'little old lady.' Call it God, call it healing, call it a miracle, call it whatever you wish. The fact is, he is fully recovered."

So ended the interview. As we were leaving, one of the doctors asked if they might interview Agnes. I said I would try to arrange it.

Agnes responded enthusiastically to the invitation. Later that week, we all met for lunch in the same clinic. There was quite a gathering: Agnes and I and a dozen or more psychiatrists and the clinic staff. Philip was not present.

The doctors questioned Agnes at length. "I am not a faith healer," she said, "but a teacher. I simply teach people how to pray as I have learned to pray. Hearts respond to prayer very well."

They wanted to know what kinds of illnesses respond to prayer. "Almost all illnesses respond to prayer," she said. "But I have never seen a severed spinal cord healed, nor do I often see arthritis healed."

One of the doctors interrupted. "I think I know why a severed spinal cord does not respond."

"Why?" Agnes asked.

"Because the spinal cord is made of the same stuff as the brain," the doctor explained, "and destroyed brain cells are not replaced. So through this sort of prayer you can't rebuild the spinal cord."

"I was wondering why that was," Agnes said.

After more than an hour's wide-ranging conversation, Agnes was asked the cause of Philip's illness.

"Philip is an extremely sensitive person who takes in a tremendous amount of fear. Didn't you notice that this happened at the time of the earthquake?" All the doctor's faces showed they were stunned at this woman's insight.

"The shock of the earthquake and the hundreds of aftershocks left Philip absolutely filled with fear. Now if fear can come in, can't it go back out again as well?"

The doctors nodded, half-smiling.

"Well, I commanded the fear to leave him. That such a command will be obeyed, one must know that it will be obeyed. One must have a sense of power.

"As you people doubtless know, I am a Christian, so I get this sense of power through Jesus Christ. How the different ones of you get it, I do not know. But you must have it. You must have the absolute certainty that when you tell the fears to go, they will go."

While Agnes was talking I was watching a rather austere, bearded psychiatrist to our left. As he listened he seemed rather restless. I was waiting for him to pounce on us and tell us that all of this was a bunch of nonsense.

After another hour of conversation, he cleared his throat. I braced myself.

"Now when we do this for people, shall we stand behind them or in front of them?" he asked. I almost yelled out, "Praise the Lord!" Agnes told him that it would be better to stand behind them for the "laying on of hands" because otherwise the personality of the pray-er could intrude itself.

Some days later I received a letter from Dr. E. thanking me for opening up to his staff and associates a whole new insight into their profession and into healing.

# Except how to make it work

Not long after Philip was healed, Agnes said to me, "You know, you ministers know all about prayer except how to make it work." Her words stopped me short. I knew that, at least in my case, she was right. I had prayed for years, but my prayers seemed to bounce off the ceiling. I often preached about prayer too, but I didn't feel good about it. It was like giving instructions on swimming when I didn't know how to swim myself.

I was raised in a very pious family. We had devotions morning and evening. I was taught to have my own private devotions, which I muddled through for years. I prayed and prayed, but nothing much seemed to happen. I concluded most of my prayers with "Thy will be done," and left it at that.

"You know all about prayer except how to make it work." Agnes hit the nail right on the head, though my theological mind was jangled by her bold, mechanistic statement. I had studied carefully Andrew Murray's *With Christ in the School of Prayer*, George Buttrick's *Prayer*, Ole Hallesby's *Prayer*, St. Augustine's *Confessions*, Leslie Weatherhead's *House of Prayer*, John Baillie's *Diary of Private Prayer*, Peter Forsyth's *Soul of Prayer*, E. Herman's *Creative Prayer*, and many other books, as well as the Psalms, Jesus' prayer life, and the prayers of St. Paul—only to find that my study taught me little about *how* to pray. I knew *about* prayer, but reading did not deepen my prayer life. Understanding the theology or theory of prayer didn't help me communicate with God. I prayed daily, but I did not know the joy of "getting through."

Now I had seen my own son dramatically healed after fervent prayer. The psychiatric community had confirmed it. Was Agnes Sanford a faith healer? What did she know, or do, that I could learn? Did she have some sort of gift that I would need before I could pray as she prayed? How could I pray so that it "worked"—or was it bad theology to even ask?

With my theological background, the whole thing seemed rather ludicrous. Were we to ask God to actually *do things* for us? Was not that being a bit presumptuous? Could we, nothing but sinners and beggars, ever come before the living God and expect him to answer our petty, selfish requests? It seemed to me that God was far too busy running the universe to be bothered with appeals of mere human beings.

What would my theological professors say if they heard I used the laying on of hands? Maybe they would push it aside with, "Vaswig is a maverick anyway." The knowledgeable people in the seminary never taught me to pray for the total healing of people. Evidently they didn't believe that God could instantly, totally heal anyone. They seemed convinced that God had turned over healing of bodies to medical doctors and healing of minds to psychiatrists and psychologists.

I, too, had often poked fun at people who prayed about everything, including my wife, whom I frequently teased as being "too pious." "Why don't you bother God with big things like salvation, or running the world or his church, or creating new stars and galaxies?" I would ask. "Why bother him about our current money problems?"

I read books about Hudson Taylor and George Mueller and Teresa of Avila and St. Francis and others, but I thought such people were the exceptions that proved the rule. They were "super-saints," very different from me. I believed that prayer could change the "pray-er," demonstrating that God answered prayer. And I believed that once in a blue moon he might step in when people could do no more. But I was sure God did not act like a global errand boy, bringing a cosmic aspirin tablet to our aches and pains or taking them away with a miracle.

The healing miracles of the gospels took place primarily in the first century. Today healing is taken care of by modern medicine, I believed, and so-called miracles of healing take place rarely and then through "neurotic," "lower income," or "unstable" people. Only with those given a special gift of healing (and I doubted there were more than a handful) could miracles take place today. I heard more and more about faith healers, but I dismissed them easily as either actors or outright frauds.

"You ministers know all about prayer except how to make it work." Those words still waited in the wings for a reply.

Agnes suggested that I begin praying for people, believing that what I prayed for was in fact being done, and using the laying on of hands as she had done. I was too afraid, too unsure, too traditional to start something like that.

"But," she reminded me, "you have seen God heal your son. Now I'm quite sure he would like you, as a minister, to pray with faith for others as well."

How in the world would I ever begin? I studied the gospels carefully, searching especially for reasons we should pray for people today when there are other solutions. For example, why not counsel them instead? As a pastor, I had tried to guide countless people to solutions to their various problems. I had been successful many times, but it was all very time-consuming and fatiguing. What if it were possible to *pray* with counselees so that in a shorter time more could be accomplished and more lasting results achieved? Or was that *using* God?

I decided to take Agnes's advice and dare to begin praying for people who came to see me, but first I had to learn more about prayer through a group experience. I asked four men from my congregation whom I knew well and loved dearly if they would join me in a quest—a quest to find out more about this thing called prayer. It would mean reading many books and spending two and a half hours together every week, at the very least. They all wholeheartedly agreed.

Our group met for the next two years. It was one of the most delightful, fulfilling experiences of my entire life. We visited Agnes a number of times to discuss and pray for the needs of our world, our country, and one another. We learned how to meditate together and often shared our needs with the group. We experienced real and powerful healings of body, mind, and soul.

During this time I got up the courage to begin praying for individuals in my church office. I had prayed for people in stressful situations before—situations I felt were too big for them or for me to handle—but I had never used the laying on of hands. Now whenever I prayed for anyone in this new way I told them immediately afterward that they were not to tell anyone. If they asked why, I said that Jesus often told people not to tell anyone when they were healed and I was merely following his example. They didn't know I was afraid people would think

I was some kind of a "kook" if the word ever got out.

I did not want to be labeled by my brother pastors as "neo-Pentecostal" or "radical" or "far out" or "on the fringe." I wanted to stay within the orthodox traditions which I cherished with my whole heart. Was it "orthodox" to pray for others? Certainly. I studied Scriptures only to find dozens and dozens of passages referring to prayers for others and to "asking" and "receiving." I rediscovered many instances where not only Jesus, but also the apostles used the laying on of hands for people who were healed.

But wait! Just because Jesus did it, that seemed no reason for me to do it. He was crucified. Should I be? Should I do what the apostles did? I'm just a nobody 2000 years later. Who am I to pray like that? Isn't it the fanatics who make the mistake of thinking there is no distance between biblical times and ours?

I was especially disturbed when I read James 5.

Is anyone among you in trouble? He should turn to prayer. Is anyone in good heart? He should sing praises. Is one of you ill? He should send for the elders of the congregation to pray over him and anoint him with oil in the name of the Lord. The prayer offered in faith will save the sick man, the Lord will raise him from his bed, and any sins he may have committed will be forgiven. Therefore confess your sins to one another, and pray for one another, and then you will be healed. A good man's prayer is powerful and effective (vv. 13-16 NEB).

I noted that the passage says those "in trouble" should turn to prayer. The ill should "call for the elders of the congregation." Did that mean the sick should call the church council or the board of deacons to pray them back to health? They would be taking their lives in their own hands, I thought. Surely all we could do would be to ask God on their behalf to heal them, quickly adding, of course, "Thy will be done," to cover ourselves in case he chose not to.

The anointing of oil scared me even more. I had heard of it before, but always in cases of terminal illnesses or accidents, and I had never heard of any recoveries because of anointing. I recalled that on one occasion we had anointed a young man who recovered miraculously, but I passed that off as being an exception.

The point in the passage that stopped me

dead, however, was: *"The prayer offered in faith will save the sick man, the Lord will raise him from his bed and any sins he may have committed will be forgiven."* What in the world is the "forgiveness of sins" doing all mixed up in the healing of the sick? I remembered Mark 2, about Jesus healing the man let down through the roof. He said to the sick man, "My son, your sins are forgiven," and then, "Stand up, take your bed, and go home" (NEB). Apparently forgiveness and physical healing were connected. Sickness was as much an enemy of Jesus as was sin.

Having read Mark 2, how could I have believed that Jesus was only interested in forgiveness and not bodily healing? Had he not wed the two inextricably? My questions were endless. Was illness God's will or was it an intruder—something Jesus opposed? Was demon possession the same as mental illness? Why did Jesus often tell people not to tell they had been healed?

The point of James 5, for me, was *"the prayer offered in faith."* What does it mean to pray with faith? Simply put, it means "believing it shall be so." It means daring to venture out and trust God. Such trust was very real to me because of an incident when I was 17.

Though I grew up in a Christian family, I was a rebellious, self-willed teenager. Ashamed that my father was a lay evangelist, I told people he was a salesman. I disobeyed my parents and often took Christ's name in vain. I chose to have no association with God—at least no willing, conscious relationship. But I became so burdened with guilt that I lay awake at night, wondering whether I would be saved if I died or if Christ should come.

One night when my father was out of town, I decided to get up and see if I could find the way back to God through the Bible. I paged through the whole book, not able to find one passage that seemed to help me. I was miserable. Finally my mother awoke. When she saw me with the Bible in my lap and tears in my eyes, she gently asked if she could help. I told her I feared I was lost and that if I died I would not be saved.

She took the old King James Bible from my hands and opened it to 1 John 1:9, pointing to the passage for me to read: "If we confess our sins, he is faithful and just to forgive us our sins, and to cleanse us from all unrighteousness."

She told me those words were written for me, that very hour. "God's Word is true, Billy, no matter what. Whatever sins you may have committed, God will forgive. God cannot lie, or he would not be God. Trust him. He will do it." Then she took the Bible and turned to the last book, which I thought no one understood. She pointed to something in the third chapter and asked me to read it: "Behold, I stand at the door, and knock: if any man hear my voice, and open the door, I will come in to him, and will sup with him, and he with me."

My mother said, "There are just two things to this business of salvation—forgiveness and Christ living in your heart. If you ask him for forgiveness and invite him back into your heart, you will be saved. You feel you have wandered away like the prodigal son, but you can come back to him again."

We got down on our knees by the sofa. She prayed for me. Then, with many tears, I confessed my sins and asked Jesus to come in and take over my heart. She prayed for me again, thanking God that the angels were rejoicing in heaven over one sinner who had repented.

Then she asked me how I felt and I said, almost hopelessly, "No different."

"How *do* you feel? Can you describe it, Billy?"

"Well, I feel kind of like I'm on a cliff and it's dark below and I don't know what to do."

"Jump off the cliff," she beckoned. My mother knew that the way to assurance was to risk all—and jump!

According to Bruce Larson, *wholeness is daring to risk danger.* That's why kids walk across narrow tree trunks above creeks. That's why teenagers dive off high rocks into deep water. They are growing up. They are becoming whole.

My mother was pointing the way for me to become whole: Risk danger! Jump! Trust that God will be there to catch you! Trust that God's Word is true. Stake your life on the fact that he will forgive your sins and come in and possess your heart.

I trusted. I believed. I risked. I moved toward wholeness. I knew that I was forgiven and that God accepted me by grace. Though I'd tried to go my own way, God had always been beside me, like the Hound of Heaven. I did not choose him, but he chose me. I did not come to him, but he sought and found me. I trusted his promise, but he gave me the faith to do so.

All this came back to me when I looked at

the phrase "prayer offered in faith" in the Book of James. It was as though God was saying: "Do you remember when you were 17? Do you remember how you simply trusted the two promises that your mother pointed out in my Word? It is no different now. You have tried all sorts of other ways, but the key is right here. Trust! Jump! I promise it, and I cannot lie. It shall be so! Don't make it so complicated. If you pray, believing and trusting, I will do it!"

I began to pray for people with the simple trust I'd learned when I was 17.

One Sunday morning after church, a member of the congregation came up to me, threw his arms around me, and with tears in his eyes told me his wife was in a very bad way. Because of a spinal problem, she had very poor circulation in her lower legs and feet. A number of her toes had been removed. The remaining toes were now infected and the surgeon said they must be removed also. I went with a man from my prayer group to see the woman.

We chatted for a time and then—with the laying on of hands—visualized the arteries to the feet and toes opening up and the toes being restored to normal health. We visualized the light and energy of God entering the woman's body and healing her completely. We held her up in our imaginations as being happy and able to get along without any trouble. Then we thanked God that it was so.

We left, thanking God that we had been able, through him, to pray for the woman. We continued to hold her up before God in the days following. I prayed for her again the following week in my office.

Not only were the woman's toes healed, but her whole person received a new, fresh experience of the grace of God. Gently and surely, God was increasing our faith.

I was called to the hospital one day by a distressed woman whose husband had lung cancer. When I arrived the man was just being wheeled from the recovery room. I met his wife and was about to speak to the man when the surgeon walked in. They had opened his chest and found his lungs so filled with tumors that they could not all be removed. He was inoperable. Inoperable!

We prayed together with a kind of hopeless optimism. I feared he was about to become one of the dozens with this dreaded disease I had buried over the years. But I felt a ray of hope. Maybe God would touch this man with healing as he had touched the woman with infected toes. Why not? Was cancer beyond God?

We arranged for prayer therapy along with the prescribed radium therapy. In a few weeks X rays showed that his lungs were perfectly clear! Whether he was healed by the radium or the prayer, I do not know. Both are gifts of God and means by which he heals our bodies.

Later a tumor appeared in the man's head. It was treated, we prayed for him the same way, and the tumor disappeared. Today the man is apparently perfectly well.

I prayed for many people during the next few months. Many times nothing happened at all. Then I would try a different prayer approach the next time. Sometimes healing would come the third or fourth time I prayed. Migraine headaches were healed, as were colitis, ulcers, back pains, asthma, and arthritis. People were also released from fear, anxiety, insomnia, impotence, guilt feelings, and loneliness.

Whether the people were healed through posthypnotic suggestion or by divine fiat, I do not know. The very first people for whom I prayed experienced movement in my hands as I prayed. They thought some sort of power was being generated, but I believed it was only because I was nervous. I still was afraid the healing was a psychological delusion or possibly even an act of the devil posing as an angel of light.

But God has many ways of accomplishing his purposes. The Bible promises that he heals all our diseases (Ps. 103:3). Gradually, as I watched him touch people with healing, my faith increased.

It was, to me, providential that Agnes urged me to pray for others first and not be concerned about my own spiritual development. I could easily have become bogged down in my own unworthiness and sin. I could easily have started taking my own spiritual temperature and found myself saying, "I'm not sure I am one who can do this anyway." If you find yourself saying that as you read, I beg you in Jesus' name to hear this. This kind of praying *is* for you. The "gift of healing" described in the New Testament may be the ability to command healing as Peter and John commanded the lame man in the Book of Acts. I'm not saying we all have this special gift. But I believe all Christians can practice the kind of healing I describe.

I learned from Agnes Sanford several keys to the praying that was now becoming a routine, integral part of my pastoral care. One was the laying on of hands. I pondered why the laying on of hands was important, and I found three essential reasons. First, Jesus did it, as did the apostles, and they commanded others (such as James) to do it also. Second, the laying on of hands brings about a physiological change. Studies by Dolores Krieger at the New York University School of Nursing have demonstrated that the hemoglobin or oxygen content of the blood is increased through touching. Third, touch creates between the pray-er and the pray-ee an intimacy which is not achieved any other way. Jesus demonstrated his love through touching.

Agnes also taught me about "healing light." I know from experience that this light exists, but it is difficult, if not impossible, to discuss it theologically without getting into extremely hazardous waters.

The word "light" often appears in the Bible, as a glance at a concordance will demonstrate. I always understood that word in the metaphorical sense. "God is light" meant he is the opposite of evil (darkness). I never thought of God sending out his "light"—a kind of real energy. Agnes Sanford has believed in God's "light" in terms of real energy for many years. In many ways her belief has been sustained by modern physics and psychology.

Biblical revelation of the concept of light begins in Genesis. As a child I wondered why Genesis 1 spoke twice of God creating light. God said, "Let there be light" in verse 3, but then went on to create "lights" in verse 4. I know of only one kind of light—light from the sun and moon and stars. Was there some other kind I could not see?

In the seminary I learned that the Genesis accounts were not scientific and that I had no right to ask scientific questions of religious literature. OK, I bought that. But the question persisted in my mind. What if the Genesis accounts were scientifically true as well? What if the author was describing the origin of something known to science, but not taken into account by theology?

Fred Hoyle, famous British astronomer, speaks of a light in interstellar space which he calls "food for the heavenly bodies." As the planets whirl through space, they leave a dark wake behind them, indicating that they absorb the light. Even the planet earth uses the light as food. But the light is not "used up" by the heavenly bodies. It is replaced from a seemingly unlimited source.

Is it not possible that when God created human beings the very life principle or energy within him was a form of light radiation? Is it not possible that God gave his children light as part of his own nature, that the light then diminished considerably at the Fall, and that sickness and even death were natural consequences of this diminished energy? I am talking about a high-frequency energy or radiation that is found all about us. It is not God, but rather a created means in which he works—a cosmic light.

If you have ever looked at a man in deep depression you may have noticed that the light appears very dim in him. When you look at a corpse you can see that the light has gone out. It may well be that in the next few years we will see modern medicine diagnosing illnesses, both mental and physical, by looking at the relative brightness of the light in different parts of the body. I believe that recent experiments with plants at U.C.L.A. and elsewhere have demonstrated the existence of this very light.

I wonder if God's hope for his Old Testament people was that the light increase in them—not only the light of knowledge and faith and obedience, but this physical light. The prophets were to make known God's

Word and recall Israel to her foundation. Was not Israel to be a "light to the Gentiles"? As light bearers they were to give the knowledge of God's glory to the whole world. The Book of Jonah is an example of their reluctance to do so.

When Israel failed, God chose as his light bearer one who said, "I am the light of the world." "In him was life, and the life was the light of men." John the Baptist was "not the light, but came to bear witness to the light." Jesus' light was divine-human, making it possible for humans to look at him and not be consumed. Jesus said, "Let your light so shine before men . . ." and John said, "If we walk in the light . . . we have fellowship with one another, and the blood of Jesus Christ cleanses us from all sin." Is it not possible that we are talking about physics as well as using theological metaphor?

A high-frequency radiation, beyond the rainbow spectrum, before ultraviolet and beyond infrared, is all around us, though not visible to the unaided eye. I have asked God to use me as a channel to conduct this light into an ill person, bringing wholeness again. I am still not certain whether light-healing is fanciful or if it is based on science, but I am certain that *it works*. This high-frequency radiation is available for channeling through humans into those whose light has grown dim in illness, whether it be physical, emotional, or spiritual. Possibly it is helpful to the imagination, which in turn strengthens faith and enables the pray-er to see the healing take place. I think it is more than that, but I won't press the point any further since I am not a scientist. I know the light is not God, but I believe it is his creation and that it may increase in a person with the laying on of hands.

Perhaps the most important thing Agnes Sanford taught me about prayer is that it has to do with imagination. I have believed almost all of my life that God comes to us through the Word and sacraments. However, I have often wondered how this happens. Precisely how does God speak to me through the Word and sacraments? Can he speak to me immediately? Does he change the synapses in my brain so that new thoughts come into being?

I always thought of imagination in somewhat negative terms. I often heard imagination disparaged: "Oh, don't let your imagination run away with you" or "That's just your imagination." Genesis 6:5 says that the imagination of man was exceedingly corrupt, and that God was sorry he had made man because of his exceedingly bad imagination.

But in George Bernard Shaw's *Saint Joan* there are a few thought-provoking lines about the imagination:

Robert: What do you mean voices?

Joan: I hear voices. They come from God.

Robert: They come from your imagination.

Joan: Yes, that is how God speaks to me.

I believe imagination is one of the most important keys to effective praying. God comes to us through imagination. If I can *see* a sick person as healthy (in my imagination), it is a short step to believing the person can be healed. Jesus said, "Whatever you ask in prayer, believe that you receive it, and you will" (Mark 11:24). Isn't believing that you receive something using your imagination and seeing it done? Whether I am praying for someone who is sick or depressed or about someone's financial problem or about a broken relationship, if I can see restoration in my mind's eye, I find myself believing that it shall be so.

Imagination was a great help in praying for the woman whose feet were healed. I don't know whether the suggestion of wholeness through prayer caused her body to respond or whether imagination proved to be only a prod to faith. But I have found imagination to be of enormous help in many other cases as well. I have learned to "see" stiff limbs moving, ears hearing, skin perfectly clear, fears and anxiety gone, and health, joy, and happiness taking their place.

One day a woman came to me in despair. Her husband, a young intern, was having an affair with a nurse at the hospital where he worked. The whole thing was about to break up their marriage. It is extremely important that both wife and husband see the counselor about their problems, but this man was not about to come in and see me. The woman was beside herself with anger, fear, anxiety, guilt, and shock. What could she do?

God desires that marriages grow and deepen and that they last. I decided to turn the problem over to him. I prayed that the woman's husband would go to work, look at the nurse, and feel shocked that he had become involved with her. I visualized him coming home and seeing his wife as the lovely bride he had married some years before. I visualized him being attracted to her in a new and beautiful way. Then in the prayer I saw a brick wall coming up, brick by brick, between him and the nurse. I visualized the old walls between him and his wife coming down, like snow melting in the hot sun.

Within a week the man accepted an offer for a new job, and the problem was settled. You may be prompted to say that the new job would have come along anyway. That doesn't matter to me. The situation was resolved and the couple has a new, refreshing, deep relationship.

Certain psychological techniques can also be helpful in prayer. While psychology does not give meaning (only religion does that), some of its teachings are valuable.

Agnes has a habit of calling the unconscious mind "Junior." Junior can be summoned to aid the visualized prayer. For example, if I am praying for a person with curvature of the spine, I suggest to Junior to carry out the perfect intent of the body, to straighten the spine. I ask the person to repeat that command to Junior daily. If I am praying about a sexual problem, I suggest to Junior that sexual energies be channeled in the right and normal areas. I visualize a river which has overflowed its banks being commanded gently to return to its natural flow. I may even command Junior in Jesus' name. If I am praying about an alcoholic problem, I suggest to Junior and to the taste buds and to the whole body that it simply will not tolerate alcohol any more. The person prayed for may then develop a violent distaste for liquor. A smoking problem can also be healed through prayer and gentle commands to the lungs to reject smoke.

The unconscious mind is like a computer: whatever goes in is what comes back out. Computer people have a word for it: GIGO (garbage in, garbage out).

We so easily program our unconscious mind in negative ways. If I constantly say aloud or even think that because many of my relatives died of cancer, it is sure to happen to me, I am programming Junior to think that way and the disease may very well ensue. If I say, "I can't remember names, but I always remember faces," I cause Junior to comply. If I say, "I hate myself," Junior will pick up that message and self-hatred probably will become a fact.

But Junior also may be programmed through positive affirmation. Negative habits developed in childhood can be broken through reprogramming — through affirmations said morning and evening in a relaxed state, to make Junior start thinking differently. For example, if I have implanted deeply in my unconscious mind the belief that I cannot draw, I won't be able to. But if I begin to affirm that it is easy for me to draw and I enjoy drawing very much, the chances are good that I will start drawing and enjoying it.

When we were living in a parsonage years ago, I tried the affirmation principle. Though we had no money in savings and had no interest in purchasing a house, I began repeating every day, "We enjoy living in our $50,000 home." In two years we owned a home, which is now worth well over $50,000. The church sold us the lovely parsonage we had lived in for 10 years for what it had cost them originally.

Was it affirmation, the caring congregation, or our prayers and prayers of others in our behalf, that caused this to come about? Probably all of these things. But I have found that the way to get to Spain is to begin collecting brochures on Spain. William James once said, "Any idea constantly held before the mind must come into existence." The author of Proverbs said that as a man "thinketh in his heart, so is he" (23:7 KJV).

Affirmations are biblical. The Word is full of positive affirmations. St. Paul said, "Whatever is true, whatever is honorable, whatever is just . . . think about these things." Also,

"Let your minds be remade and your whole nature thus transformed" (Rom. 12:2 NEB). And is not Jesus Christ the very "yes" of God?

To affirm the great commandments by repeating them and setting them deeply into the unconscious mind is to do what the psalmist said: "Thy word have I hid in mine heart, that I might not sin against thee." Is not the repetition of the Apostles' Creed a seating deep into the unconscious mind the truth of the faith? Memorizing scripture passages and prayers provides fortifications against the onslaught of evil. To strengthen me for walking in the light, I constantly affirm "I believe that when I ask, God forgives me through Jesus Christ and that he immediately forgets my sin forever."

# *Daring*
# *to become whole*

Alfred North Whitehead's concept of the "prehension of all things" gave me insight into the nature of prayer. The universe is like a lake into which a stone is thrown. Ripples move out from the center to the outer edges of the lake. Everything in the universe is connected in some way to everything else.

This helped me understand for the first time that, for good or for ill, there is no such thing as a solitary life. My deeds and deeds of other people affect the entire universe. My anger can express itself a thousand miles away in war. My love can be reflected in a caring act by my neighbor. The good or evil I do to others, they tend to repeat with someone else.

I came to understand that my words are but the smallest part of prayer. My deeds are the essence of my relationship to God and therefore my total prayer. A person of prayer must live in harmony with the divine will. The essence of prayer is living in a loving relationship with God.

Because of my upbringing it was difficult for me to think of God as a loving Father. While my stoic, Norwegian-born father surely loved me and my brother and sisters, he was afraid to express affection. He was very slow to anger and usually said nothing rather than cause pain, but we wanted him to *talk* to us. I remember how disappointed I was that he never placed the car keys into my hand, but always dropped them into my hand as though I were untouchable.

When I first read in the New Testament that the promises in Jesus Christ are the "yes" of God, I wondered if my father knew him. Father said "no" to whistling, "no" to sports, "no" to movies, dancing, cards, and lipstick, "no" to words like "shucks" and "heck," and "no" to cutting paper on Sunday because that was "work."

At a very early age I began to think that God was a "no" man, against almost everything on earth. I thought he must be angry,

silent, brooding—a killjoy who didn't want
me to have fun and certainly didn't want me
to laugh. My mother projected another kind
of God to me, but father's view had more
force. After all, wasn't he a preacher? Didn't
he know what the Bible taught about God?

Once near Jerusalem I heard a young boy
running after a man crying, "Abba! Abba!"
I recognized it to be the Aramaic word for
"dad" or "daddy." I almost never called my
father "dad." He was too austere, too distant,
too formidable. Neither did my father or we
children—up to the point of my father's death
—ever think of God as "daddy" or "dad." He
was too "high and lifted up," to quote Isaiah.
We were filled with awe and reverence in his
presence, but seldom with love and warmth.

When my father died, what surprises
awaited him! Although he knew the grace of
forgiveness of sins, he never knew the grace
of a loving relationship with his heavenly
Father. He never felt accepted for who he
was. He never knew a father who was close
to him or expressed deep caring for him. But
now that he was home with Christ, he knew
that God was not a "no" God but rather a
"yes" God—loving, graceful, kind, affirming.
What a revelation! Once in my imagination

or a dream, I found myself in the heavens where I found my father absolutely delighted with the God he had found.

In some ways I am deeply grateful to my parents for the concept of God they passed on to me. It was far superior to some watered-down conception of God as ever-loving grandfather, willing to overlook anything. But after my father died, my angry caricatures of God dropped away. I began to perceive a God of love who really cared for me.

I learned that God loves me just as I am, "warts and all," as Martin Luther once said. At age 40, I was discovering that God not only forgave my sins, but loved me and wanted to communicate with me. He wanted an open, alive relationship with me.

The late psychologist from Brandeis University, Abraham Maslow, outlined five levels of communication. We relate to many people on the cliche level, the most shallow level of communication: "Hi, how are you?" "Fine, thanks. How are you?" The first person doesn't really want to know and the second person doesn't care to say. Much communication is on this level, partly out of necessity.

On the second level of communication, two people speak of a third person or thing. When two people talk about their pastor,

congressman, president, neighbor, teacher, or
employer, in either a positive or negative
way, they are on the second level of communication. People who are afraid of depth
tend to stay at this level. They can only talk
about others.

On the third level of communication, two
people talk about a subject such as politics,
economics, religion, or the weather.

The fourth level is arrived at when I begin
to tell you who I am. When I share with you
my hopes and hurts, my pain and my joy, my
neurotic feelings and my highest aspirations,
I give you the gift of my self, the gift of love.
Some people seldom discuss their inner lives.
Over many a grave site where husband and
wife are buried side by side, the gravestone
could well read: "Here lie two people who
never knew each other."

The fifth and deepest level of communication is reached when you come back and tell
me who you are. When you return my love
by giving me the best you have—that is, your
self—we have reached a "peak experience,"
moving personal communication. We tell
each other our deepest secrets. We want to
be known and want someone to know us.

Any of these levels of communication may
describe a person's communication with God.

How easy it is to stay on the first, second, third, or fourth levels. But God wants to know who we are and to tell us who he is. Though in his wisdom he already knows us well, he wants us to communicate with him. He wants us to tell him about our belief and unbelief, joy and sorrow, hope and hopelessness, love and hate, tears and laughter.

The best gift I can give God is to tell him who I am. That means confessing my sins—my pride, my selfishness, my unlove, my smallness. It means telling him about my world and its pain and sorrow and meaninglessness, and telling him that I want to change, but cannot unless he enables me. It means telling him I am filled with the wrong goals, with misplaced hopes and false security. I acknowledge that I can never come to him except that he calls me and bids me come. I tell him I love him. I call him "Abba." I praise him and thank him and adore him. I believe that he loves and accepts me and that I am a child of the King—a son of God!

Once I tell God who I am, he will communicate to me who he is. The Bible is the record of God's revelation to his children, climaxing in the Word that became flesh. God also reveals himself to me. He comes to me in the personal relationship called prayer. I talk to him and he talks to me through his Word and sacraments by the power of the Holy Spirit. The Word and sacraments have direct impact on me. God communicates with me as a person. He touches me in at least six ways.

*God touches me thorugh my imagination,* as I've already discussed. Imagination is one of the keys to the relationship of prayer with God.

*God touches my mind.* He can and actually does put ideas into my head, as he did to biblical writers. Their writings are more inspired and therefore more authoritative than mine because of their proximity to Jesus. They were eyewitnesses; I am not. No matter how moving may be my experience of God, it will never match in depth or significance the experience of those who walked with him and witnessed his resurrected glory. Yet, God touches my mind.

*God touches my emotions.* He touches my negative emotions with his mercy and love. He turns my loneliness into solitude, my hostility into hospitality, my hate into love, and my illusions about morality into prayer.

I have learned to trust my feelings more. I used to put everything through the gristmill called intellect and will. If it couldn't be figured out with my rather limited mind, it wasn't worth attention. But now I place more trust in my "gut" feelings, and I'm no longer afraid to let my feelings show. I can cry now, for example, though I used to think it unmanly. I can praise God more freely. When he touches my "praise button," my heart fills with gratitude.

*God touches my will.* He gives me the will to do something that pleases him. For example, I never thought that I would be writing a book. I didn't want to write a book. Here I am writing and enjoying it. Fears cross my mind as I write. I fear what theologians are going to say, among other things. But God has given me the will to do it.

When I was 13, some guys dared me to steal from the local dime store. I walked in, confident on the outside and scared silly on the inside. I looked around. I made my way to a counter, reached over the glass, and slipped something about six inches long into my pocket without even looking to see what it was. When I got to the street the guys were waiting. I pulled out the "loot" from my pocket. It was a golden-colored ruler inscribed with the words: "Do unto others as you would have them do unto you."

For years the thought of that ruler haunted me until I finally wrote a letter of apology to the store and sent money in payment. It took *will* to write that letter. He touched my will.

*God also communicates to me immediately through memory.* There would be no Christian church if it were not for memory to keep past events contemporary. The Christ who *was* is the Christ who *is present.* Holy Communion is meaningful because we remember him. The Bible is the memory of the people of God.

Finally, *God speaks to me through my body,* the temple of his presence. He speaks to me clearly about my needs through my body, though the speech is often in the negative voice of illness, my body telling me loudly, "Something is wrong!"

Illness is an enemy, an unnatural intruder. Our loving God does not cause illness. He has programmed the body for health. He redeems or edits illness so that good may come from bad. The body miraculously heals itself by his power. When you cut your finger, the cut heals itself. Stitches, bandages, and medicine only enhance the process. When you break your arm, the body knits the broken bone back together. The doctor just sets the bone and puts it in a cast, to permit it to heal properly. As the psalmist says, God "heals all your diseases."

When I began to pray for the bodily health of other persons, I discovered that often all I did was help remove a barrier so God would enable the body to heal itself. Accident victims often were healed very fast following prayer, because fear or whatever hindered the healing process was removed through prayer.

I had always believed in the forgiveness of sins since I understood the name God. As a child I also believed God could and would listen to my prayers. But when I grew older I became convinced that God was busy minding the universe and gathering his church, and that he could provide only generally for my welfare. Now I know the God who forgives my sins also cares for the temple of the Holy Spirit called my body.

Many of us acquired from the early Greeks the belief that the soul is imprisoned in the evil body, and it gets what it deserves since it was only "clay" anyway. We presently need a kind of ecology of the body, which will deliver us from the concept of "soul salvation" into the concept of "whole salvation."

Once when I prayed for a man with a physical ailment, I was startled to find that he was converted to Christ. Far more than physical healing took place in his life. The one who touched his body also touched his whole person. God was not interested in *only* his body or *only* his soul. Healing is a way God uses to make the redemption of Christ real!

My deepest perspective on daring to reach out in prayer for the needs of others came through a tragic but valuable personal experience. In the summer of 1974, for no apparent reason, my ankles swelled up. I went to see three internists, one of whom specialized in cardiology. Each doctor took an electro-cardiograph, but none of them made a clear diagnosis. They also analyzed my blood, which seemed normal. But my ankles continued to hurt badly, so I stayed home from work.

My wife, Marcine, had a routine checkup that week. Just in passing, she mentioned my problem to her doctor. He exclaimed emphatically that his professional friends didn't know what they were talking about and that I had better see a vascular surgeon immediately. That afternoon I took his advice. The surgeon's diagnosis was angina pectoris and blood clots in the legs. He put me in the hospital immediately.

The doctors said I was less than a week away from a major, if not fatal, coronary occlusion. Two arteries in my heart were more than 90% occluded and the third, more than 80%. My dear friend Agnes came and prayed for me before the final diagnosis had been made and told Marcine she felt as though I would have to go through something extremely difficult before this was over. I was put on a blood-thinning drug, and in three days, after a heart-catheterization, I was scheduled for open-heart surgery.

This time I faced possible death. The prayers had done their work and nothing had changed. Now the surgeons were about to do theirs. God would use them to bring about life, whole life. A sister in the Roman Catholic hospital asked me if I was ready to meet God. My surgeon made the sign of the cross over my body before surgery. I discovered that the medical profession is God's tool for healing. I gained new appreciation and respect for all my nurse and doctor friends, whom I now see as servants of the Lord.

After some six hours in surgery, my first recollection was in the intensive care unit. A nurse was cleaning my battered body, which had been cut, sawed, wired, and sewn. Three coronary bypasses had been performed. Veins from my legs were now supplying my starved heart with rich blood.

The healing process was slow, especially because I greatly feared any problems concerning my heart. My sore rib cage stimulated the memory of my diseased heart every time I moved. I feared dying. I feared being alone. I feared never being able to go back to work. I feared the long, hard recovery.

What was it all about? God had shown me that whether he uses doctors, medicine, surgical techniques, or prayer, he is the healer. He was to do something as significant in my life as he had done in Philip's. In a year I would know what it was.

In three months I was back at work. How sensitive I was now. I had been brought low to the grave. I hurt all over. I cried often and became very sensitive to pain—mine and others'. I had to walk at least three to five miles a day and I became much more aware of nature.

I also became more sensitive to children. On my walks, for the first time I really got a look at children other than our own. When Jesus said, "Except you turn and become like children, you will never enter the kingdom of heaven," I thought he meant we should be humble like children. But what is humility?

Is it a kind of "I'm no good—glory be to God" piety? Does it mean forever saying, "Thanks for letting God use me" in an attempt to give God glory for a good sermon? Does becoming like a little child mean announcing that I am nothing but sin and shame? Does it mean acknowledging that "I am all mud" but "my Savior is all grace"?

This is not at all what children do. Children recognize and are not afraid to say who they really are. They are not pompous. They speak the truth in a straightforward way and in love.

The significant characteristic of children, which I think reflects their humility, is their openness. Openness is rare among adults. How open am I to the experience of the neo-Pentecostals? How open am I to other theologies, and how bound am I to the traditions of my own church? Have I developed blind sides to my thinking?

At weddings I sometimes hold a picture before the bride and groom at the altar and ask them what they see. I have often heard the groom say one thing and the bride say the exact opposite. If they believe that only what they saw is there, they lock onto one truth and lock the other out. All of us see only partially, and a child is willing to admit it.

I have developed love for children also in learning to pray for them. Many times I have prayed for children who disturb classrooms, and they respond rapidly. Most children who constantly harass teachers do not need spankings. They probably have already had enough of those. They need someone to take them on their lap and pray for them.

Usually I pray that God will cause the little child to see himself as accepted and as a worthwhile person. If praying for a little boy, I often ask him if he ever hit a home run or more than a single. If he says yes, I ask him if he remembers how happy his teammates were. Usually he remembers very well. So I ask the boy to picture himself rounding third base with all his friends cheering him on and loving him.

Then in my prayer, I ask God to quiet down the little storm within him and help him to see himself as a loved, neat kid. Almost without exception such prayers help the child very much. Since it is easy to get back into the old patterns of behavior, I may pray for the child again within a week and then in two weeks and again after a month.

I also have learned to pray for asthmatic

children in a way that has proved helpful. Asthmatic children are often very hostile and have a good deal of anger inside. According to a recent theory for treating asthmatics, they are often helped by a "parent-ectomy." Parents of asthmatic children are often very caring and deeply devoted to their children, but many times they need to give the child more breathing room, more "space."

It is important to teach the child how to breathe, how to relax, and how to recognize the signs of an asthma attack. In prayers for asthmatics, I visualize the tiny microscopic sacks in the lungs being flooded with the light of God's presence. I see the little collar around each sack becoming relaxed and the air flowing in and out easily. I see the child able to express anger and I pray that the parents will allow that to happen.

I love to pray for children because they are so open. They possess real humility. I have prayed for children with all kinds of illnesses, often with considerable success.

My good friend Agnes was instrumental in another answered prayer that happened, and is happening, in our own home and which has given me great courage to be more open to what God wants to do.

Agnes and her good friend Edith were at

our home one evening. The previous week our pediatrician had discovered that our daughter Rene had scoliosis, curvature of the spine. She was sent to a child's orthopedic surgeon who was reputed to be the best in the San Fernando Valley. After a thorough examination and X rays, it was determined that Rene had an 18% curvature and that the spine had curved in two places. We were told that she had to be fitted with a $700 Boston Brace, which she would have to wear constantly, day and night, for at least two years.

The night Agnes visited, I asked her, just in passing, if she would please pray for Rene's spine while she was there. During the course of the evening she took Rene to a bedroom in our home and prayed for her. She asked Rene when the problem seemed to have begun and where it was located. Rene reached back and put her hand on the top of her spine between her shoulder blades. Agnes prayed and then gave Rene instructions about affirming a straight spine in the mornings and the evenings.

The next week the doctor surprised us by remarking that the top of the spine was now straight but the bottom was as crooked as it had been. We inquired and discovered Rene had asked Agnes to pray only for the top.

When we saw Agnes again, I kidded her about only doing half the job. She asked what I meant and I explained what had happened. She took Rene back to the bedroom again and this time prayed for the whole spine.

When the doctor X-rayed Rene's back during her next visit, he was shocked. He asked the therapist how long the brace had been on. "One week," was the reply. The doctor called in two other doctors. The X ray hanging before them now showed only 1% curvature. From 18% to 1% in just two weeks!

Now you may believe, as the doctors believed, that it was the brace that changed Rene's back. That might be so. I'm quite sure there was much more involved, however. To me, our prayers were answered.

You ask, "What about those backs that don't straighten out?" I don't know why some people are healed and others are not. Only eternity will answer that question. One factor seems to be empathy between the pray-er and the pray-ee. In counseling, empathy is more important than knowledge of techniques, and it may be equally important in prayers for healing. Jesus often touched with healing those to whom he was moved with compassion. As a pastor, it was almost incumbent upon me to pray for everyone who asked, but the healing seemed to go more easily with persons I cared for.

Absence of healing apparently has nothing to do with lack of faith. Sometimes a person of strong faith prays and there is no healing. But that doesn't mean we should believe our daughter's back was healed by "chance."

I am certain God wants us whole. If Jesus were walking physically on the earth today, would he not want the sick with whom he came in contact to be made well? I just cannot see Jesus saying to my daughter, "Rene, it is my will that you have curvature of the spine all your life. It will help you trust me more." The notion that illness is the will of God is *heresy*. "Healing the sick" was not something that happened in addition to the gospel. *It is part of the good news!*

So often when we pray for a person's health we use "thy will be done" as a "copout," as an escape hatch—just in case. We should pray "thy will be done" with assurance that God wants the person whole. It is extremely important to thank the Lord that he has heard our prayer and is already beginning to answer it.

God allows certain things to befall us, it is true. I'm sure that my heart problem passed before his eyes. He permitted it to happen to me. The chances are that I suffered because of the way I went about my work and my "God-almighty attitude." I needed to be brought down to size. I suppose he permitted the cholesterol to build up in my arteries to the point where surgery was mandatory. But he did not actually cause me to get sick nor does he want me to continue to be sick.

A year and a half after surgery I began to have angina pectoris again. My heart was apparently demanding more blood than it was getting. Another heart-catheterization showed an artery which had occluded 25% at the time of surgery was now—only a year and a half later—almost 90% occluded. I was still in the way of having a heart attack. The cardiologist thought it would be "light," but he wasn't sure.

That news, together with the continued pressure of a large, suburban parish, greatly increased my anxiety and thus the probability of heart attack. I was popping nitroglycerin tablets every three or four hours. Things got heavier and heavier for me, to the point where I thought I was going to die very soon.

One day my district president, whom I love dearly and who is a great pastor to pastors, dropped in to see me. I told him that I was, that very day, writing my resignation from my parish. "I'll die if I stay on this treadmill any longer," I said. After he listened to me for about an hour, he agreed.

I decided to form a small, nonprofit corporation called Preaching and Prayer Ministries, to venture out with no salary whatsoever to conduct evangelism and prayer missions across the country. Two months after my new work began, the angina had decreased greatly. Now, many months later, I seldom have any angina. In recent "stress tests" on the treadmill the doctor was convinced that the "lateral flow" has begun and that I will not have the predicted heart attack.

God wants me whole. He did not cause my illness, and he is editing history so that blessings come forth from it. I praise God every day that out of Philip's illness and my own heart problems, we have entered into an exciting, fulfilling new ministry which is providing increased wholeness. Not long ago I kidded Philip that I should have left the parish ministry five years ago, to which he replied, "But Dad, you would have never met Agnes and I would have never seen the inside of a nut house." Out of the two worst experiences in our lives God has brought about the best that has ever happened to us.

# *Prayer in church*

Many of us Christians have all the gifts of God, including fruits of the Spirit, but the gifts remain all wrapped up, as if they are still in the closet. God gives us a new automobile with a full tank of gas to take us on our journey through life, and we end up pushing the car. We try our level best to do it on our own because we don't know it can be done any other way.

Discovery of these gifts, all of a sudden, is like an explosion. How exciting when a congregation which has been pushing the car on its own strength for years suddenly realizes that the powerful Spirit desires to do the work for them. (That is not to say that all we

Christians need to do is sit back and pray. On the contrary, we must serve our brothers and sisters in the world, motivated by the graciousness and love breathed into us by the blessed Spirit.)

But, you ask, how can I discover the gifts wrapped up and waiting in my closet? Ask someone to pray about it with you. "Every one who asks receives." Paul's admonishment to "earnestly desire the spiritual gifts" simply means to be open to receive whatever God has to offer you. The gifts, in the main, are natural gifts which God supernaturalizes so they may be used in his kingdom. They can be released in the local church and in individual lives through the worship service. They can be released in your life.

Plan to arrive at the church at least 10 minutes before the worship service is to begin. Instead of talking up a storm with everyone around you, concentrate on the auspicious Guest who is present. The Lord of all glory has promised to be at all gatherings in his name: "Where two or three are gathered in my name, there am I in the midst of them." We have his word of honor—believe him!

Visualize the presence of the Holy One filling the sanctuary. Hold before your mind the vision of Isaiah in the sixth chapter. Visualize the light of God's presence coming down like a cloud of light, similar to the pillars of cloud and of fire that led the Israelites. Visualize Jesus standing in the chancel with hands outstretched in blessing. Repeat gently the words, "Come, Creator Spirit."

Allow your mind to move freely and gently from the cross to the altar and to the general architecture of the sanctuary. Rejoice that we have beautiful places in which to worship. There was a reason Moses received long and detailed instructions regarding the tabernacle. Something about the colors and furnishings of a church speaks to the deep mind. Much more is taking place during these moments than we can ever imagine. Modern psychologists tell us that we receive millions of impulses into the brain every second. How good to be in a place where the prayers of God's people have been prayed and where the building is literally saturated with his holy presence.

Turn your attention to the pastor or worship leader. Ask that the "power at work within us" fill the pastor and the gathered congregation. Do not pray that the pastor will say what you want to hear. Rather pray that God will heighten the preacher's ability to boldly proclaim God's word. If the pastor says something which offends you, you are generally safe in believing it was God's word of judgment to you that day.

Fortunate are the pastors who are so prayed for by their flocks, that the offensive as well as the comforting aspects of the gospel will be clearly spoken and heard every Sunday morning! Every preacher whose congregation is devoted to such prayer is truly blessed.

The four other men in my prayer group made it a point to be in church early and to hold up both the congregation and the pastors in prayer. I always found it extraordinarily strengthening to catch their eye on Sunday morning and know that they were praying. Because of it I dared to be faithful to the text, to let the Word speak even if it meant some squirming in the pew.

One Sunday a professor of philosophy told me that if the congregation really knew what I was saying in my sermon that day they would not tolerate it. "They think you're too good a guy to really mean it," he quipped. But I believe many of them did know what I was saying and they gave me the freedom to say it. Only God knows what controversy

I was spared because of the prayers of those four good men.

Pastors today are badgered and beaten by the winds of secularism and pluralism. They need their congregations' support. Trying hard to be faithful to their high calling, most preachers are very self-critical. They need less criticism and more encouragement. If congregations would realize that most of a pastor's life is public and therefore open to criticism, and that the pastor is very much aware of this fact and is probably afraid of it, they would go light on criticism and heavier on supportive prayer.

This does not rule out divergence of opinion. Informational criticism (not personal attack) is necessary and helpful. But it is nearly impossible for a preacher to give Christian direction to the flock in one hour without the prayerful support of the congregation.

After remembering the leader of the flock in your prayers, look around the congregation for the person who looks as if he were having a gall bladder attack right then and there. Ask the love of Christ to come through you and into him to comfort him. Ask that the unhappiness that shows on that person's face may be healed in the worship that day.

Imagine what would happen on Sunday mornings if even half of Christian congregations spent 10 minutes before worship in prayer. God's children would experience his divine grace. Bodies, minds, emotions, and souls would be healed in great numbers.

Sunday announcements generally describe individuals in need, buildings to be built, outreach to be accomplished, and inreach to be shored up. The worship service provides time to pray about these concerns. During the communion service, instead of watching everyone else go to the front, how about remembering in prayer the church council, the Sunday school teachers, the choir, the organist, the evangelism committee, the stewardship committee, or the women's groups?

Take someone in your mind up to the communion table with you as a special concern. Especially remember the sick. Visualize the light of God's presence surrounding and filling the person who is ill. Imagine Jesus Christ himself in the hospital room, bringing healing and wholeness. Visualize people flocking to your church because of the warm fires of love burning there. Visualize every home surrounding the church being filled with the love of Christ.

Praying about financial concerns is legitimate and correct. We can pray that God, who owns all resources in the world, will give congregations the gift of giving. I do not think we can be apologetic about suggesting at least a tithe in the church. I was once a bit gun-shy when it came to asking for money because I felt I was asking people to give to "my" programs in "my" church. How absolutely wrong I was. Is it not Christ's church? If we ask what he wants, should we then be afraid to ask him to lay giving on the hearts of his people? If stewardship committees would spend as much time praying about finances as they do on programs to raise income, I think more money would flow in more easily.

I know of a congregation that prays about financial matters, and many members give not only a tithe, but a double tithe. Be specific in the prayers about money. **Ask the** Lord for specific amounts and then trust that it will be so.

If you decide to form a prayer group, ask five or six persons to join you. Such groups easily degenerate into gossip-factories, so determine at the outset that you won't let that happen. Don't pray for your aunt in Florida whom no one else knows. Choose four or five topics of concern to everyone and stick to those. It is not necessary for each member of the group to pray about each item. One can articulate the feelings of all, at least generally. If you disagree about a subject, drop it from your prayer list. It is important to be "of one accord and of one mind."

Instead of always praying in your home or at church, go to hospitals where your friends are and share a prayer with them in person. All the effects of the laying on of hands are readily available. Simply hold the hand of the patient and put your other hand on the patient's forehead. The love communicated through prayer is especially encouraging to one who is ill. Why not let ill persons experience your prayerful concern for them?

We need to pray fervently for our nation. At one time this land seemed limitless in its acreage and its opportunities. We thought that we were the new Israel, the people of God in a land of milk and honey. We had our own Moses (George Washington) and our own Abraham (Lincoln). We believed that we could not fail. What more could a nation accomplish than to land men on the moon? Poets, preachers, and philosophers for years warned of our "dark side," but we failed to listen. We pressed forward to conquer.

During the 1960s we discovered some sad

facts: oppressed blacks and disenfranchised Indians, pollution, violence, urban shambles. Today America faces an identity crisis. Is this the new Israel after all? Will Americans continue to press forward, leaving the "weak" to rot where they fall? Will we maintain the arrogance of power that shouts, "We will be the first and the best in everything, regardless of the cost?" Or will we face who we really are?

I believe the opportunity is now at hand for us to become what God intended us to be. We are ripe for change. There is much good in the American dream, but we need to retrace our steps, truly seeking "justice for all," and correct the mistakes we made along the way. This is the time to heed Jeremiah's words: "Stand by the roads, and look, and ask for the ancient paths, where the good way is; and walk in it, and find rest for your souls."

And how we need to pray for our leaders! Although government is ordained by God for the sake of the gospel, there are strings attached. Pray that all of our leaders may realize that their power is to be used according to the will and purpose of God. Visualize Christ the Lord, the Ruler of nations, in your city, state, and national council chambers.

Pray that his will be done on earth, as it is in heaven.

Pray too for other nations, and for the evangelism needs of the church. I implemented many good evangelism programs in the course of 20 years in parish ministry, but most of them lacked one thing—they were not steeped in prayer. If Christ is the real evangelist, why not pray that he will open the hearts of people to the invitation to attend church and come to faith? More specifically, pray that he will lead you to the person to whom you can effectively witness, and pray for knowledge of that person. Leave it up to the Lord to open the doors, and witness at his arrangement. He has a timetable, and his Spirit will prepare the way.

I have found that people do not need to be preached at so much as they need help to find meaning in their lives. People are wandering in a morass of meaninglessness. Viktor Frankl, after being imprisoned in a Nazi prison camp and witnessing the destruction of fellow Jews, said, "There is no healing without meaning." The Master can give a sense of meaning and bring healing. When you witness to what the Lord of Glory has done in your life, you witness to the possibility of meaning for another. Support your witness through prayer.

One of the significant turning points in my theology of evangelism came when I let the parable of the judgment of Christ in Matthew 25 really speak to me. On my first trip through the parable, I was somewhat surprised to find no reference to any creed. Those on trial were not charged with any crime or with breaking any commandments. The test was simply kindness — ordinary, down-to-earth kindness such as feeding the hungry, clothing the naked, and visiting those in prison. It seemed to me on first reading to offer ammunition to the humanist who says, "Isn't that what we've been saying all along? Just love your neighbor."

But in a thorough examination of the text, all sorts of selfishness is exposed. Much more than human decency is required. Even the saints fall far short.

We dare not be complacent about others' needs. The condemned group thought they were good enough. "When did we see thee hungry?" The text focuses on a profound moral paradox: the less good are characterized by a complacent conscience and the spiritually sensitive are tormented by their own unworthiness.

Nor are we to be socially selective. Those who passed the test were all-inclusive in their sympathy. Their compassion was not limited to their own family or circle of friends or their middle-class church. They reached out to the despised. Jesus crashed into the cozy establishment world and reversed their scales of values. He taught that publicans and prostitutes may be nearer than religious leaders to the kingdom of heaven.

Jesus was also very severe with conventional Christians for their selectivity. We approve those who dress like us, speak like us, and support the same causes we support. We may even approve of the socially inferior, as long as they approve our superiority. Jesus was "not impressed." What about the misfits, the riff-raff, the scum, the alcoholics, the divorced, the homosexuals? The words that strike home are, "As you did it not to one of the least of these. . . ." "Least" is the key word. All of us stand under the judgment of Christ.

Christians are not to remain uncommitted spectators. Christ's grounds of rejection are not crimes against humanity, not moral ineptitude or heretical beliefs. *He condemned those who did nothing.* They were judged

because they sat in the grandstand and refused to get involved.

"Not everyone who says to me, 'Lord,
Lord,' shall enter the kingdom of heaven, but
he who does the will of my Father who is in
heaven." Evangelism is not just reaching
souls, but reaching out to the needs of the
total person. Such evangelism is no empty
emotional experience, but rather a radical
implementation of Jesus' words.

# *Your deepest hurts can be healed*

Our lives are a unit from conception to death. More and more embryologists and biologists have become concerned with what happens to us in the first nine months of our lives. They are demonstrating to our amazement how quickly the implanted ovum responds to modification from the environment —the perfect sphere already pulsates when it is implanted in the uterus.

Current studies demonstrate that we respond to our environment from conception. In fact, we are totally permeated by it, sharing the molecules found in the world around us. Embryologists are now saying that at conception we "recapitulate the life of the species."

We used to think of the womb as safe, bump-proof, thermostatically controlled — almost a perfect environment. It is now common knowledge that babies in the womb know their mothers' voices, respond to light, and react to noises outside. They experience their mothers' moods of joy or fear through body chemistry which charges through their blood as well as through their mothers'. Prenatally we can experience both traumas and happiness, which may and often do affect us for life.

The environment into which we were born was not safe and loving. The generation of our parents and their parents before them created a persecuting environment which we must enter at birth. The sights, smells, sounds, tastes, and touches of a modern antiseptic hospital are generally the exact opposite of what babies would choose if they had the knowledge and ability to do so. This environment is not only unpleasant, it is harmful.

Hospitals are equally unpleasant for adults. Though the word "hospital" means place of hospitality, patients are assaulted by drugs, kept from their dear ones in the most difficult hours, unable to eat home-cooked food or listen to their favorite music, isolated from small children.

In *Medical Nemesis* Ivan Illich shows how we have completely medicalized illness. We are all now in what he terms the "world hospital." Seven percent of people entering a hospital today with no disease will come out with one. If we don't drop dead on the streets, we are caught in machines to live on as vegetables in the environment of death. Rarely can we die at home.

The persecuting environment we have created in hospitals we construct in a different way for our institutions of learning. To Plato education was drawing forth the gifts of another. His method was asking questions. Didn't he ask an ignorant slave questions that brought him all the way to geometry? We frustrate learning by giving answers before there are questions; we give our children crutches before they have learned to walk. Students are expected to merely regurgitate in examinations the facts they've been programmed with. We never let them grapple with real questions.

We have also created a general environment that is destructive. Like people in a room into which poison gas has been slowly filtering, we are deluded about our safety.

But we have learned, like the carp in Lake Erie, to adapt our lives so we are able to survive pollutants.

Our nonphysical environment is hostile also. We are surrounded by hate and anxiety. Because there is anxiety there is fear, and where there is fear there are always implications of danger. What are we afraid of? We could answer with a long list, but the single thing we are afraid of most is one another.

The healing of the memories can dissolve the hurts of such an environment. I have witnessed children and adults, teenagers and the very old healed through the laying on of hands and prayer for the healing of memories. Prenatal memories registered on an infant's brain, still open wounds after many years, can be healed through prayer. The soreness around the memory of a breech birth or some other birth complication registering deep in the mind can be touched with healing through prayer.

Painful or even hateful days at school, when failure and defeat were the lot, can be touched by Christ and healed. The fears and anxieties so common to us all can be cast out or lifted off through prayer for the healing of memories. I have watched healing take away terror induced by *The Exorcist* and by a holdup. Pain caused by divorce of parents or alcoholism in the family or death of a loved one can be touched and healed years later by the Master's hand.

The concept of healing memories originated bout 20 years ago with Agnes Sanford's prayers for Harry Goldsmith. A Czech Jew, Harry immigrated to America as a young man and became a naturalized citizen. Agnes first met him in the "wet ward" of an Army hospital, where soldiers were due either for death or for high amputations. Harry had been wounded in action. His left leg, which was filled with shrapnel and osteomyelitis up to the hip, and he had lost six inches of bone.

Although it was against hospital regulations, Agnes would pray secretly for anyone who was willing. This young Jewish man had no prior knowledge of prayer at all, but he was extremely sensitive, and he realized as Agnes prayed that something was happening to him and his leg.

Agnes soon taught Harry how to pray for his own leg, visualizing the bone being rebuilt and visualizing himself walking again. She did not make the mistake of preaching at him, but it wasn't long before Harry realized that someone he chose to call "the other

One" was at work in his life. In six weeks his leg was healed. The doctors could not believe what they saw. Surely there was a mistake—it must be someone else's X ray.

Harry went up and down the ward telling everyone about his miraculous healing and about this amazing experience called prayer. He even spearheaded a time of silent prayer in the ward during afternoon quiet time. Everyone would begin with the man at the door and pray silently for each man in turn.

Some weeks after Harry was dismissed, Agnes found him back in another ward, in traction. "What in the world are you doing here, Harry?" she asked.

"I was kicking a football and my leg broke."

They chatted awhile. Then he said, "I have a feeling you have something to tell me. Come on now, what is it?"

She agreed that there was. She said the reason she had not spoken earlier was that in many ways Christians had not been very good to Jews, including blaming them for the death of Jesus. Agnes left Harry a little story by a man named John. The next week Harry said he'd had to read it two or three times to get the hang of it, and that he had a question to ask her. "Is that who the other One is?"

"What do you mean, 'the other One'"?

"I mean that when I pray for my leg I feel like someone else is with me."

Agnes agreed with him nervously. "Yes, I have no doubt that *is* who the other One is."

Then she left him the gospels of Matthew and Luke, somewhat afraid that the stories of the virgin birth, angel choirs, and Wise Men would turn him off. But the next week he told her, "If I who am nothing and know nothing can build six inches of bone back into my leg through prayer, it is nothing to believe that his birth should be surrounded by such strange events. Of course I believe it!"

After Harry was discharged, he paid Agnes a weekend visit. She tried to persuade him to enter a sanctuary with her. He was anti-church, but reluctantly, he agreed. When they entered the rear of the sanctuary, he exclaimed, "It's here!"

"What's here?" replied Agnes.

"The power that heals. Can't you feel it?"

He was later baptized and confirmed.

But soon quiet, sensitive Harry became a very angry person—so angry that he once threw water at people and tossed a typewriter on the floor. He wrote to Agnes, "You have places for people like me in this country," referring to mental hospitals. He could not control his anger.

Agnes asked the Lord what it meant, and it came to her that it was not the grown-up who was angry—it was "little Harry." As a Jew, Harry had been mistreated by the Germans. He was physically beaten and shoved around from concentration camp to concentration camp. As a young boy he was unable to respond appropriately. His persecutors were too many. He was too little.

Healing was taking place in his physical and spiritual life, but his emotional life needed healing also. The anger repressed for years started erupting like a volcano. The deep cuts made at five years were now spewing pus out at anyone around. "He needs a prayer for the healing of those memories," thought Agnes. She took him as her special concern in her imagination and heart to the communion table, praying for the deep healing of the mind of the little boy, still very much alive in the young man.

Later he wrote Agnes and asked, "What have you been doing?" He experienced complete and lasting healing of his youthful memories. He is now a psychologist whom

I have heard lecture at a school for pastoral care.

That is how Agnes began praying for the healing of memories, with amazing results in the lives of thousands.

The chief purpose of Jesus' life on earth was our atonement by his death on the cross. Isaiah, hundreds of years before it happened, put his finger on this unfathomable mystery in these words: "Surely he has borne our griefs and carried our sorrows." Somehow through his suffering he was able to bear our griefs and carry our sorrows—not only our *sins* but our *griefs* and *sorrows* too.

Paul describes Christ's accomplishment even more profoundly. "He made him sin who knew no sin, so that in him we might become the righteousness of God." Jesus actually became sin for us. He took our sins into himself and suffered the penalty, that we might receive what he is and has.

Gethsemane may help us understand how God heals memories and why it is possible. Jesus brought 11 men with him to the garden. Eight stayed back while three entered the heart of the garden with him. He fell on his face in anguish. He cried out to his Father for removal of the cup—not because he was running away. Rather, he was like a mother in labor crying "Please help me," though she wants to have the baby.

Through this struggle, as blood mixed with sweat and dropped to the ground, Jesus opened himself to the sins of the world. He opened his psyche to the "collective unconscious" (Jung's phrase) of all humankind from the beginning to the end of time. He opened himself to all the griefs and sorrows and sins of every person in the history of humanity. All the wars and crimes and immorality of the entire human race he absorbed, to take it to the cross. The cup he shrank from drinking contained the poison of all our sins, which would surely kill him. He who knew no sin became sin for us—the fear and terror and despair and cruelty and brutality of all humanity absorbed by the one God-man for us all.

Jesus bore it all to the cross the next day amidst the brutality of the soldiers and the violence of the scoffers. His first words were a prayer that the people be forgiven because they did not know what they were doing. When I realize that he died not to only forgive me but to heal my griefs and sorrows, I am filled with anticipation for myself and for others.

When Philip became ill, psychiatrists and

psychologists tried to probe for causes. They turned up some interesting clues. When they asked if he was ever alone under unusual circumstances, we recalled an incident when Marcine was pregnant with our second child. Philip was playing in the basement where she was washing clothes. She started hemorrhaging. Philip witnessed an ambulance haul his mother away bleeding. Weeks later in that same basement he put together his first three words in a phrase: "Mommy, I scare!" Fear at such a young age can have a profound effect on a person's life.

When Agnes prayed for Philip the second time, she prayed for the healing of his memories. She prayed about his life in his mother's womb and about his birth, asking the Lord to erase any fears that still resided in the mind of the boy now grown up. She went through his whole life with him and with us, to learn what events might have left sorrows or griefs.

Then she visualized Jesus Christ, unbound by space or time, going back to the time of the particular hurt and healing it. She prayed that the soreness around all the wounds of the past would be healed. She visualized Jesus comforting and holding Philip, healing the deep hurt and filling his life with perfect love. The healing Philip experienced was perfect and complete.

We feared that going back to the psychiatrist would reopen the old healed wounds. I was amazed and gratified that Dr. E. believed what had happened and never tried to stab open healed wounds.

I have prayed the prayer for the healing of the memories for hundreds of people, both privately and with large groups. In almost every case, it has been a deeply healing experience. In a group led by Francis Mac-Nutt, I sensed a deep healing as he took us back to the very womb where we were formed. I have seen a woman suffering fear and anxiety after a robber held her at gunpoint for three hours instantaneously healed through prayer for the healing of her memories.

In another incident, two girls home alone heard a gunshot and a thump. They found their mother dead at the door—shot in cold blood. The memories of that experience lingered for years. Through prayer for healing of the memories, Jesus soothed them both. He went back in space and time, deep into their minds, and he bore their griefs and carried their sorrows.

People in deep emotional trouble because

of horrible childhoods can be helped through healing of memories. I have often prayed about people raised in horrendous homes and have seen quite rapid healing.

I'm not sure how such healing occurs. Maybe spoken prayer releases suppressed sorrow so it no longer hurts. Maybe God touches in a deeply profound way the mind of a person. Surely if he can say, "I will remember their sins no more," he can also cause someone I am praying for to remember the hurt no more. I don't care exactly how it is done. I just know that it works and that it works almost every time. Praise God!

At a recent mission I prayed for the healing of the memories at the end of a lecture. A few days later I received the following unsigned letter.

Pastor Vaswig:

Words can't really express my thanks to you for bringing your healing ministry to _____. Even though many of us sat through your lectures without showing much emotion, we were deeply touched by everything you said (if my own experience is any indication).

Your prayer for the healing of the memories meant a great deal to me.

Four years ago, my husband and I decided to end an unwanted pregnancy by means of abortion. This happened at a time when we hadn't been attending church and did not feel close to the Lord. (We are both Christians by heritage and infant baptism, but only recently are asking the Lord to take over in our lives.) By some unspoken agreement, we never talked about the abortion with each other over those whole four years! No one else in our family or circle of friends knows about it, and I didn't feel I could discuss it with a minister that I have to face regularly.

I have been carrying around a tremendous burden of guilt all this time, but I felt the love of Jesus lift it from me last night. All through your prayer, I prayed for the same healing for my husband, who was not at the services. When I came home, he was in a very receptive mood (he tends to be a grouch sometimes). We talked about it for the first time—not agonizing over it, but claiming the forgiveness of Jesus. It was super! We've never felt so close to each other or to Jesus.

# *Learning to meditate*

We were sitting in the sand at the beach watching the waves come rolling in when Agnes remarked, "Let's pray, shall we?" Before long we had not only spoken to God, but were off to the highest heavens listening to him.

Sound eerie to you? That's OK—three years ago I labeled such things dangerous, subjective, unbiblical, or a waste of time. But that day I learned from Agnes something more about prayer that I shall never forget. I discovered contemplative prayer as a form of Christian meditation.

Meditation is not always Christian. In fact, centers of non-Christian meditation are springing up all over the United States. It seems that the nation leaped from the active '60s to the meditative '70s in a single bound. Americans, who once turned outward, got tired of crises and disasters and they suddenly turned inward, away from the "artificial," "alienated," "inhuman," "materialistic" world to a search for selfhood.

Having gained the world and apparently lost their souls, Americans are undergoing an identity crisis. As the churches emptied in the late '60s, the clinics filled up in the '70s. Carl Jung became high priest, and people looked more and more boldly into their "deep side."

Non-Christian meditation is primarily an inward search for access to the deep self, while Christian contemplation is only partially a journey inward to the self and primarily a journey outward, away from self to God.

In our hunger for experience today, thousands are getting "turned on" to "alpha breaks." Thousands of others are turning on to Transcendental Meditation, which, though in the garb of religious neutrality, is religious through and through. While there may be some aspects of TM recoverable to Christians, surely the repetition of one of eight or nine secret mantras naming a Hindu god won't be indulged. We can learn much from the East, but we must be extremely careful lest in uncritical acceptance we swallow something poisonous.

We need contemplation because we need to "shut up and listen." We have talked too much and too long. How many of your own acquaintances can tell you of an experience of the sense of awe and wonder they have experienced lately? Most of us are missing this vital aspect of religious experience. We attend church, say our prayers, give our money, and attend meetings, unaware that there is something gripping and earthshaking in the faith we hold. We do not experience the holy, the totally other, the presence, the numinous—we do not experience God.

Trouble in the church has been ascribed to many causes: materialism, "future shock," the rise of science and technology, apathy about social issues, and Western rationalism. There is some truth in all of these explanations, but more important is our loss of the experience of awe and wonder.

Awe is the experience of becoming aware that one is in the presence of the ultimate reality of the universe. It is experiencing something or someone altogether else. It is

encountering a reality totally beyond humanity. We stand before a mystery never to be
understood.

How does contemplation help us recap-
ture the experience of holiness? Through contemplation we become like Moses before the
burning bush, or the children of Israel before Sinai, or Isaiah on hearing his call before the throne of God. During contemplation, as during the transfiguration, the veil
between the seen and unseen world grows
thin. It is like seeing a New Testament miracle take place before our very eyes.

Our secular age has placed its trust in
technology. We have not been able to con-
ceive of levels of reality beyond the immediately perceptible, far less explore them.
But the answer may come through science
itself. Looking at the microcosm today,
scientists say that there is no bottom to reality and that each new discovery does not
diminish what they do not know. While I
learned in college that atoms, neutrons, pro-
tons, and electrons were the bottom rung of
reality in the microcosm, scientists now know
of at least 26 levels below that.

The same is true of the macrocosm. Scientists now say there is no end to the galaxies;

interstellar space is increasing faster than the speed of light. Planets are undulating into nothingness, while new ones many times the size of earth are being born every second. There are large holes in space into which heavenly bodies pass and disappear. That fills me with awe.

Humanity is also a mystery. People ran off with the pieces of the puzzle before we had the picture put together. We don't even understand the physiology of our own brain. The handful of pinkish grey jelly which puts together 10 watts of electricity and some chemicals and 13 billion cells and comes up with a theory of relativity or a sonnet—that fills me with awe. I realize that I *am* not a body, nor do I merely *have* a body. Only because of the Fall did I become aware that I had a body. Only because of sin do I see my soul and body as separate.

Once while my family was taking a trip across Canada, we visited Banff. Never in my life before or since did I react as I did when I saw Lake Louise in all its splendor. I simply could not breathe. I experienced breathless wonder, and I was very much aware of the Creator's mighty hand. Looking at mountains and caves, vernal fields and roaring rivers, lakes and the mighty Pacific often fills me with a deep inner quiet. "Be still, and know that I am God," said the psalmist.

Somehow I have experienced the deepest sense of awe in suffering. I stand amazed before my own suffering and the suffering of others. God takes something apparently evil and turns it around for good. Suffering has a way of cleansing and purging, and though God seldom or never causes it, it passes before his eyes. He is in my suffering and I am not alone. When death is but a handsbreadth away, one becomes terribly conscious of God's divine lordship. The experience of suffering fills me with awe.

Preparation is necessary before contemplation begins. At a pastors' meeting, I heard Agnes expound on Psalm 24:3-4. "Who shall ascend the hill of the Lord? And who shall stand in his holy place? He who has clean hands and a pure heart, who does not lift up his soul to what is false, and does not swear deceitfully?" Historically, the psalmist is speaking about the journey up the hill to the temple where worship would take place.

But his words are equally significant for preparation for contemplative prayer. "Who shall ascend the hill of the Lord?" Who shall draw near to the throne of grace? Who shall meditate? Who shall be still to know that he is God? Who shall dare to stand on the holy ground of contemplation? The one who has "clean hands" and a "pure heart." Nobody has clean hands in the sense of a sinless life. No one has a pure heart in the sense of absolutely selfless motivation.

But "clean hands" means willingness to let go of every sin. "If I had cherished iniquity in my heart, the Lord would not have listened." If I harbor a grudge or nurse hatred or continually cheat the government, I cannot expect to ascend the hill of the Lord. Not only would I not be able to contemplate, but I would be endangering my own emotional and physical health. Something cannot be morally wrong and emotionally healthy. To have a "pure heart" is to "will one thing," according to Søren Kierkegaard. To "will one thing" is to desire above everything else what God wants. Let him be Lord! I can't even do that, however. All I can do is to be honest with God and openly confess to him, and then let him do it.

Before I meditate, I always do three things I learned from Agnes. The ritual theologically is based on Ephesians 6:13-17. We put on the armor of God to shield ourselves against anything evil which could harm or mislead us during the contemplative prayer, and during that day. Paul says, "We are not contending against flesh and blood, but against the principalities, against the powers, against the world rulers of this present darkness, against the spiritual hosts of wickedness in the heavenly places." I do not want to take the chance of contemplation without first shielding myself against the attack of the evil one.

After seating myself in a straight chair, I say, "I sign myself with the sign of the cross." As I say it I make a large sign of the cross over my body. There is nothing magical about that—it is a symbol for the deep mind. I am sealing myself with the cross of Jesus. I need to know that daily.

Then I say, "I cover myself with the blood of Jesus Christ," and I pass my hands gently over my head and shoulders and most of my body. I see myself, not covered with red blood, but rather under the power of the energy given off in the shedding of Jesus' blood. I remember the story about Luther at the judgment seat of Christ. The devil accused him of sins which no one knew anything about, but which the devil was going to announce. Luther quoted the familiar passage, "The blood of Jesus Christ cleanses me from all sin." As I prepare for contemplation, I see myself cleansed in the blood of Jesus.

Finally I say, "I circle myself with the light," and I draw a circle four or five feet in diameter around me. This light is the shield of God's presence which the evil one cannot penetrate. Then I make all three signs for each member of my family, visualizing each of them in their own setting, wherever they happen to be.

After letting God wash my hands and purify my heart, and then having sealed myself with the three symbols (the cross, the covering of blood, and the circling with light), I am ready to listen. Then the conscious mind becomes the problem. It flits here and there, picking up this forgotten message and that task to do today. A necessary step is "centering down," or being still, quieting the conscious mind. I often sit in the backyard and look at the trees. Brain studies show that green and yellow are the best colors for issuing alpha or relaxed brain waves.

William Glasser talks about jogging as an excellent means of centering down. Some meditators recite a secret mantra. Others suggest the use of a mandala, a cross or other symbol, or a picture to quiet the mind and settle it down to God. If you have the gift of speaking in tongues, this is the time to use it. The purpose is to somehow quiet the conscious mind so you can "be still and know."

Sometimes to center down I repeat the "Jesus prayer." Some years ago, when Agnes was in very deep depression, she repeated over and over: "Lord Jesus Christ, Son of God, fill me with your light and your love." Years afterward an Eastern Orthodox priest told her the words were very similar to the Eastern Orthodox "Jesus prayer." I first heard of the Jesus prayer through Henri Nouwen's *Reaching Out*.

I was delighted to find *The Way of a Pilgrim*, by an unknown author, in a bookstore one day. It tells of a Russian peasant who traveled about trying to discover how to "pray without ceasing." After months of travel from church to church and monastery to monastery, a "starets" or teacher told him to say the Jesus prayer: Lord Jesus Christ, Son of God, have mercy upon me. He said the Jesus prayer 3000 times a day, then 6000 and then 12,000. Finally the prayer of his mind moved down and became the prayer of his heart, and he prayed the Jesus prayer in rhythm with his heartbeat. He had learned how to "pray without ceasing."

The great "Hospodi Pomilui" which the

Russian Orthodox choirs sing as the cross is lowered to the center of the chancel on Good Friday, is whispered when the cross is down in place, but the music reaches a mighty crescendo as the cross is raised.

On the beach the day I learned contemplation, Agnes and I shielded ourselves and prayed for protection. Then we played a little game. We imagined ourselves out in the lovely calm ocean water lying on our backs in the warm sun. Then we imagined ourselves being lifted, soaring to heights unknown by us before. We went past sun and moon and stars. The air was cool and absolute quiet prevailed. We were still so God could speak.

I didn't hear any audible voices that day or any other day. But is there any reason why God cannot speak to our inner minds today just as he has done in days gone by? Maybe the word I hear inside will be a reminder to do something. Maybe I will see something very beautiful. Maybe I will get clear advice about what direction my life should take. Maybe a word of God from scripture will pop into my mind with new clarity and meaning.

For a beginner, contemplative prayer is very difficult to sustain for even five minutes. It becomes easier through practice. It helps me to slowly repeat: "I want to hear you, Lord, I want to hear you."

Another way I have learned to bring my attention to God is to visualize the presence of Jesus with me. His word of honor is, "I will be with you." He does not lie. I can use my sanctified imagination to visualize his presence with me as a real person. I give him the attention I would give any person in the room. I speak to him about everything that comes to my mind in these first stages, and I ask him questions.

Maybe my experience with contemplation is from intuition or imagination, or maybe it is nonsense. I don't know. But this I do know. To be able to sit, with full protection, and contemplate our Lord and sense his near presence and his directing hand, means everything to me. I yearn for the simple presence of God, for a personal understanding of his word, for knowledge of his will, and for the capacity to hear and obey him.

In my work as traveling prayer-teacher, I often stay in motels. Motels are lonely places. When you've seen one you've seen them all. I have been so lonely that I've sat and cried. But I invariably turn to God, walk through my loneliness in contemplation, and become aware of his presence in the room with me.

"Lo, I am with you always, to the close of the age."

In meditation the first ideas for the outreach program which became the Shepherd Center came to my mind. "How can we serve you best?" I asked. "Telephone" was the word that came through to me. Six years later, more than 73,000 calls for help have come in from people dialing 340-LIFE, the hotline number.

In meditation I have come closest to other human beings, closest to nature, and closest to God. I have been filled with absolute joy beyond anything else I have ever known as I sat alone contemplating God. I have lost myself in him. I have found myself in his truth.

St. Augustine once asked himself, "What do I love when I love thee?" He gave this answer: "A kind of light and melody and fragrance and good and embracement of my inner man, where there shines into my soul what space cannot contain, and there sounds what time snatches not away, and where there is fragrance which no breeze disperses." I experience something of that in contemplation.

Rabbi Abraham Heschel, whose life was a

serving one if it was anything, was balanced by deep spiritual experience. He wrote:

> A moment comes like a thunderbolt, in which a flash of the undisclosed sends our dark apathy asunder. It is full of overpowering brilliance, like a point in which all moments of life are focused on a thought which outweighs all thoughts ever conceived of. There is so much light in our cage, in our world, it is as if it were suspended amidst the stars. . . . We are penetrated by His insight. We cannot think any more as if He were there and we were here. He is both there and here. He is not a being, but being in and beyond all beings.

The year after he graduated from college, the Quaker mystic Rufus Jones was in France near the foothills of the Alps. He writes:

> I was walking alone in a forest, trying to map out my plan of life and confronted with issues which seemed too complex and difficult for my mind to solve. Suddenly, I felt the walls between the visible and the invisible grow thin and the Eternal seemed to break through into the world where I was. I saw no flood of light, I heard no voice, but I felt as though I were face to face with a higher order of reality than that of the trees or mountains. I went down on my knees there in the woods with the same feeling of awe which compelled men in earlier times to take off their shoes from their feet. A sense of mission broke in on

me and I felt that I was being called to a well-defined task of life to which I then and there dedicated myself.

Meditation or contemplation sets the stage for doing the deeds of God. It is the launching pad for action. It is the waiting necessary for empowering. It is the wood for the fire. After contemplation, I have read scripture in such a way that the pages seemed aflame with fire.

I now know that the most important engagement I have on any day is that appointment with God, because as Henri Nouwen said: "I see spiritual life not at a retreat from the world, but as being set free to be in the world with power."